BRAND ANARCHY

BRAND ANARCHY

Managing Corporate Reputation

Steve Earl and Stephen Waddington

B L O O M S B U R Y

First published in Great Britain 2012 by

Bloomsbury Publishing Plc
50 Bedford Square
London WC1B 3DP
www.bloomsbury.com

Copyright © Steve Earl and Stephen Waddington, 2012

A CIP record for this book is available from the British Library.

ISBN: 9-781-4081-5722-0

This book is produced using paper that is made from wood grown in
managed, sustainable forests. It is natural, renewable and recyclable. The
logging and manufacturing processes conform to the environmental
regulations of the country of origin.

Design by Fiona Pike, Pike Design, Winchester
Typeset by Saxon Graphics Ltd, Derby DE21 4SZ
Printed in the United Kingdom by CPI Group (UK) Ltd, Croydon, CRO 4YY

To

Saskia, Alfie, Ivan and Sarra

Dan, Ellie, Freya and Katie

CONTENTS

ABOUT THE AUTHORS

Steve Earl and Stephen Waddington have worked together since the popular rise of the Internet and the dawn of digital media. They've helped brands such as the Associated Press, Cisco, *The Economist*, IBM, Tesco and Virgin Media to manage their reputations.

Their views are formed from 20 years spent working in one of the most competitive media and public relations environments in the world.

Most recently they launched the award-winning Speed Communications, which has rapidly become one of the UK's most prominent public relations agencies, working with clients across conventional, digital and owned media. Both were journalists who turned to public relations and so have seen from both sides the massive upheaval in the media we consume.

You'll find the pair on Twitter: Steve at @mynameisearl, and Stephen at @wadds. After reading this book, please do share your views on modern reputation management challenges through the conversations taking place in all forms of media using the hashtag #brandanarchy.

We look forward to debating these issues with you.

Steve Earl

Steve (@mynameisearl) is a trained news journalist who went into public relations in the infancy of the Internet boom in the mid-1990s. He has handled national and international campaigns for some of the world's largest brands. He co-founded Rainier PR, which is now Speed's technology team, in 1998, having worked for two large public relations firms, Brodeur and Weber Shandwick. Steve holds a Diploma in Newspaper Journalism from Cardiff School of Journalism, and specialised in newspaper reporting, government and media law.

Stephen Waddington

Stephen (@wadds) is a former journalist who moved into public relations in the early 1990s to work with British technology start-ups. He has consulted some of the world's largest technology brands and is a regular commentator on and public speaker on public relations, in particular on digital communication techniques. He sits on the PRCA Council, the CIPR Council and is a member of the CIPR's social media panel. Stephen co-founded Rainier PR, which is now Speed's technology team, in 1998, having worked for Brodeur and Weber Shandwick. Stephen holds a BEng (Hons) in Electronics from the University of Salford.

ACKNOWLEDGEMENTS

We'd like to formally acknowledge and thank the following people that have helped inform our thinking during the writing and development of Brand Anarchy.

Mark Adams (@cluetrainee);
Richard Bagnall (@richardbagnall);
Richard Bailey (@behindthespin);
Charles Bell (@thistoomustpass);
Rob Brown (@robbrown);
Dominic Burch (@dom_asdapr);
Alastair Campbell (@campbellclaret);
Lisa Carden;
Michael Chaplin (@michaelchaplin2);
Neil Chapman (@najchapman);
Margaret Clow (@executivetyping);
David Cushman (@davidcushman);
Greg Dyke;
Cliff Ettridge (@cliffettridge);
Russell Goldsmith (@russgoldsmith);
Andrew Grill (@andrewgrill);
James E. Grunig;
Dan Howe (@danhowe);
Neville Hobson (@jangles);
Dan Ilett (@danielilett);
Francis Ingham (@prcaingham);
Peter Kirwan (@petekirwan);
Howard Kosky (@howardkosky);
Quentin Langley (@brandjack);
Barry Leggetter (@barryleggetter);
Antony Mayfield (@amayfield);
Adam Parker (@adparker);

David G. H. Phillips (@davidghphillips);
Michael Regester;
Howard Rheingold (@hrheingold);
Phillip Sheldrake (@Sheldrake);
Jonathan Simnett (@westfour);
Andrew Bruce Smith (@andismit);
Jeremy Thompson @jeremycthompson;
Mike Walsh;
Sally Whittle (@swhittle);
Will Whitehorn;
Daryl Willcox (@darylwillcox);
Ross Wigham (@rosswigham);
Heather Yaxley (@greenbanana);
and Philip Young (@mediations).

INTRODUCTION

There is a simple reason why you should not waste your time wondering whether you have lost control of your brand's reputation.

You have never had control of your brand's reputation.

Think about it: you may have been able to control everything your employees think, say and write about your brand. You may have gained – through investment and persuasion – similar influence over the media. Even all your customers might think the sun shines forth from you.

And then someone you didn't count on walks down the street and mouths off about you. 'I hate Brand X,' they say. 'I had a bad experience with those guys, gather round and I'll tell you all about it.' And they do.

That has always been the case. Since the dawn of commerce, probably. Now the Internet is taking that mouthy pest and multiplying it. A billion-fold. Worse still, those statements are immortalised digitally, can gather their own moss in a digital sense and can be seen by anyone, anywhere.

Reputation is not just under siege, the ramparts have been utterly breached.

This isn't a particularly rosy picture, is it? To top it all off, no one knows whether it's going to get even worse: will conventional media become a rapidly dwindling factor as newer, social forms of media immerse brands and hold them in a vice-like grip?

Our bet, and it is only a bet, is no: because although the nature and value of conventional media is changing, it will always have the trust factor on its side as it conveys information to the public. At least, it will if it plays its cards right.

But if you're going to try to understand what action plan you need in order to protect and develop your brand's reputation in the future, you must first understand and continue to chart media change.

Moreover, your business doubtless has a structure, a team and processes for managing reputation that are matched to the requirements of conventional media, perhaps with a little social media specialism tucked neatly to the side. Like the mint sauce next to a roast lamb dinner.

That must change quickly, or you're really in trouble.

You will never have complete control over your brand's reputation. But you might, just might, be able to get more control over it than you've had in the past. That's what this books covers. It is not very long, and even this introduction is pretty short.

Because you don't have time to waste.

CHAPTER

1

CORPORATE REPUTATION

Can reputation ever be controlled? And does the pursuit of the science of influence hold clues? #brandanarchy

'My reputation grows with every failure.'

So said George Bernard Shaw, a man with a reputation for being quotable.

In a world in which companies can shine brightly, quickly, but fade faster, and where rapid technological change leads to new ways of marketing, consumers are confronted with increasing amounts of information, each and every day. As a result, positive brand reputation that cuts through the huge swathes of information now available has never before been so highly sought after. Nor has it ever before been further from a brand's grasp.

Pace of technological change has caught the practice of reputation management on the hop. Which has many brands very scared. Hang on a minute – brands are scared? Surely it's the people running those brands who are scared?

Fair enough. Without getting picky though, think about what a brand is: at its purest level, a brand is a connection between an organisation and its customers. The reason people running organisations are scared is that their brands – those connections – are no longer 'connected' to customers by a relatively small number of tried, tested and predictable routes. Today, those connections are multiplying like nobody's business. They're everywhere, meaning the relationship between brands and customers looks really complex, at least on the surface of it.

There's no real telling how many marketing messages the average consumer in Britain is now exposed to each day. Many experts reckon that advertising messages alone number around 3,000. As digital media, in particular social media, gives customers greater and more direct exposure to brands (and as media and technological kit continues to proliferate) that number will only grow.

This probably isn't news to you. You're probably thinking that the snowballing of media began when we moved beyond four television channels in the UK; that the game changed when Internet access surged, and that we then hit warp speed when the ability to self-publish online took hold. All true. For brands today, though, the fear factor comes not just from media volume and direct engagement with customers, but from pace: the speed at which information spreads and influence is created. Both good, positive influence and the bad – negative influence on brand reputation.

It's frenetic. Brand owners may go to bed with healthy reputations but wake up to a disaster scenario. A global slanging match about a brand can happen during a tea break. And if a response plan isn't whipped up and put out immediately, all you can do is watch and weep.

Control in far simpler times

So, tough times for brands. In a simpler age, things were far more straightforward. While rarely scientific, media was established and work could be done to build reputation progressively by securing positive publicity that 'said' the right things; better still, at the right time. Negative publicity could be countered by responding on behalf of the brand, ensuring positive exposure soon followed or ensuring the information never saw the light of day.

Sound a bit like propaganda? It's easy to see why, and in the early days of what is now the public relations profession, the term 'reputation management' was coined as a way of PRing the public relations industry – as propaganda had a nasty whiff, particularly given political events in Germany before and during World War II. Propaganda was about nations being collectively swayed by the broadcasting of messages that served a purpose, typically a dodgy one. Putting it more kindly, propaganda was about a systematic and purposeful approach to persuasion, exploiting the media to do so. So put that way, the parallels with public relations come into sharp focus.

Ironically, the ability of brands to influence customers through digital media by engaging them directly can also be seen as a systematic and purposeful approach to persuasion.

But we have by no means come full circle. Rather, media has exploded in complexity, reach and sophistication, meaning the connections brands now have with customers make a pure propaganda model, as it existed in the 1920s and 1930s, impossible to sustain.

Just ask China.

Appliance of science

Realistically of course, the vast majority of brands have, over the last 80 years or so, sought to manage their reputations through techniques that are, largely, socially acceptable and which do not cast a long shadow over the very reputations they are striving to enhance. They have taken an increasingly structured and sustained approach to public relations, although media change in recent years has seen many brands adopt opportunistic, short-term and in some cases irreverent approaches too. In many cases, as in the advertising world, simply attempting such things can make brands be perceived as fresh, innovative and 'cool' by some audiences, so that alone justifies the means.

It's worth briefly touching on the early days of public relations, and in particular zoning in on what happened when brands first came to appreciate that what they said and did in public, particularly those actions that were interpreted and disseminated by a waiting media, and which could sway reputation. And, therefore, commercial fortunes.

There have been many books written about the early days of public relations, mostly focusing on the industrialisation of the United States, the emergence of public relations as distinct from advertising or promotion, and the need for a shrewd approach to managing the perceptions of customers and the workforce through what was written in the media. Perhaps the most seminal transition in those early days was from public relations being all about defending brands that had done bad things to being all about building brands of which people thought of highly. Until then, most public relations practitioners had worked for large corporations, and were largely tasked with diffusing negative situations by giving press highly-controlled access to information, in order to sway the resulting articles.

The phrase 'the media' was not in widespread use until the 1920s. During the 1930s, despite the majority of news management being war-related propaganda, pioneering brands and individual consultants began applying what is best described as social psychology in order to persuade broad target audience groups to change their behaviour – principally, their buying behaviour.

This is all interesting stuff, but the agenda was typically to get people to buy more of a certain type of thing; not get them to regard a certain brand more highly. Sales were an immediate by-product of the collective social action, rather than sustained brand reputation being the primary objective.

That notion of collective social action points to the backgrounds and beliefs of some of PR's earliest practitioners. Many had studied psychology or, what would become regarded as, sociology. They were highly interested in the reactions of individuals or groups caused by transmitting information to them in such a way that drove word-of-mouth between them.

Provocatively, by today's standards, many saw not just commercial but cultural benefit in what amounted to the manipulation of audiences through what was then a relatively primitive media.

Pioneers like Edward Bernays, who worked as a press agent for US President Woodrow Wilson during World War I, sought to bring psychological techniques to bear upon so-called public persuasion campaigns through what was seen as an 'engineering of consent'. So, something that later became seen largely as an art form stemmed from pioneers who had science front of mind. Similarly, Ivy Lee's early campaigns sought to bring a structured, planned approach to public relations work. Convincing clients that they needed to listen to their audiences as well as disseminate information to them was one of his mantras, even if techniques for listening were far less advanced than today and critics believed it was seldom put into practice anyway. Lee is lauded as focusing more on crisis communications work that supressed negative information by preventing it from becoming public knowledge through the media.

Ethics and morals to one side, one thing that PR's forefathers did was illustrate to large corporations the importance of this form of communication, and that several guiding principles should be applied in order to do it successfully. In Lee's eyes, these were that the business or, as we now typically look at it, the brand, should always tell the truth. It should always seek to provide accurate facts about itself and its operations, whether of its own volition or in response to information requests from the public or media. And the person ultimately responsible for public relations within the business must have direct access to the person who runs the business overall.

Even in those early days then, there was an acceptance that brands could not ultimately control every element of how they were perceived by the public.

Seeking more than fragile influence

Compared to today's diverse media and companies' ability to influence customers rapidly through the Internet, this early work can seem pretty primitive. Yet one thing sticks out as a factor that has remained true throughout PR's relatively short history, and has relevance today: there was ultimately no control, but brand perception rested on turning a fairly fragile relationship with customers into a more robust one, by doing and saying things that would get written about by the media, in order to get them talked about by customers. Subtlety was critical, but most important of all was to understand the context – to understand how customers would react to the information and how that was likely, or in some cases practically certain, to influence their perception of that product or issue.

In its own basic way, public relations in the 1930s was founded on establishing a dialogue of trust, understanding and respect with customers. Only then could it use that position to further the ambitions of brands to sell things and gain customer support and loyalty.

Little could those pioneers have imagined that one day that dialogue could be so direct, with new types of media forever changing the rules of the game. Yet with an even more fragile hold over influence with the public.

To delve into that, let's consider what public relations actually is. Despite it having been an established industry sector in the UK for the best part of 50 years, and despite its undeniable role in influencing editorial and, therefore, brand reputation, a consistent definition of public relations remains hard to come by. Search online for 'what is PR?' and you'll be confronted with a sea of different responses. High up the list is that of the Public Relations Consultants Association (PRCA), which states that it is 'the result of what you do, what you say, and what others say about you'. A tool used to gain understanding. Meanwhile,

Wikipedia cites it as 'a field concerned with maintaining public image for high-profile people, organisations, or programmes'. A field concerned, indeed.

So, definitions of public relations remain as vague as ever. And that's fair enough, given the broad remit of the craft and the fact that, whichever way you look at it, public relations has spent the past decade or more trying to work out what its value will look like in the future while struggling to address technological advances that have changed how influence is created.

What is PR these days?

In the meantime, the advertisers – themselves locked in the most tumultuous period of modernisation they've ever had to deal with – have realised that while they face threats, as well as seek new opportunities, because of the ability of modern media to connect directly with audiences, there is scope for the ad men to get their hands on public relations budgets. There has long been power in aligning advertising and editorial campaigns that aim to sell products or services, so audiences are being made aware and influenced through bought media content around the same time that they're being made aware and influenced by earned media content – the editorial that is driven by public relations efforts. But, increasingly, advertising agencies have found themselves competing directly with public relations agencies, and vice versa, as media modernisers and budget-hungry executives make the case that 'the line' is no longer blurred; rather, there is no line.

But most seasoned PRs and advertisers see it differently. To them, the disciplines are different because each is seeking to elicit a different kind of reaction from, or influence over, the audiences. The challenge and the opportunity is that as audiences increasingly connect directly with brands (and even actively seek some form of participative relationship with them), planning the delivery of the content, and assessing how best to gain the right reaction from the audiences, has become really complicated.

According to Mike Walsh, a highly experienced advertising man and the former European chief executive of Ogilvy[1], PR's main challenges lay not in finding its place in a changing media and marketing world, but in creating positive reactions for brands rather than defending them against negative ones. Walsh is optimistic about the prospects for PR becoming more valued as techniques modernise, but feels it must shed some of its old methods in doing so. 'PR spends far too much time reacting to crises and negative headlines. Its big opportunity has to be to get itself on the front foot in the way that it enables brands to communicate,' he says.

PR, in his estimation, is a marketing craft going through an uncomfortable period of change as opposed to being on the wane. Apart from an observation that the tag 'PR' is sometimes stereotypically associated with journalism (and so the industry needs to better clarify both what it does and its potential), public relations remains a potent weapon in the right hands. The level of transparency now being brought to bear by media change means that integrity and credibility are absolutely vital if editorial, in a broader sense, is to drive influence more forcefully for brands.

But the point here is not that public relations must be more tightly defined; it is that the way in which public relations applies itself to reputation challenges through fragmented and diverse media – media as we knew it, social media and branded or owned forms of media needs closer scrutiny.

---

1   Ogilvy UK Group: www.ogilvy.co.uk

The changing editorial world

PR still 'lives' in the editorial world. That is how it has its influence on reputation. It is still about getting someone else to say it's good rather than saying so yourself. But the editorial world is changing rapidly which means that the way public relations creates influence and tackles things that impinge on influence have to change too. Fast.

The biggest single driver in this change, fairly obviously, is the Internet. Some might say it's social media and, yes, the ability of individuals to bypass the conventional media and engage with brands directly is unprecedented. But the Internet has changed publishing forever, which has, in turn, changed both conventional and social media forms forever.

In some ways though, the role of public relations is little different to how it was during the embryonic days of the 1930s, and is far less clumsy. In fact, the industry is having to embrace techniques well beyond media relations as it modernises and this is, in effect, a return to the true, expansive public relations of those early days when multiple routes to influence were pursued, albeit in simpler times. Public relations remains something of a middleman between brands and the editorial outputs that influence their reputations. Just as the world of brands has expanded to encompass new entrants, including elements of the public sector, public initiatives and many more facets of the corporate world, so editorial output has expanded. Beyond the myriad of text, image and moving image-based content that conventional print and broadcast media now offer, media in its broader sense now encompasses all guises of social media and the branded media stuff that bridges the divide. And it's a divide that is rapidly closing.

Originally, PR's role as it became an established industry was, at its most simplistic, to befriend the small handful of journalists who wrote the most influential stuff, and come up with cunning ideas for both managing likely bad news and highlighting goodness. A crass perspective perhaps, but media relations was the thrust of it all. Over time, as the media grew and became more sophisticated, PRs had to get to know many more journalists, plus other influential people; in addition they had to try to make measurement of public relations spend more incisive, comparing it, where appropriate, to advertising spend. But back then, we were still sending 200 copies of every press release to a big list of recipients and clients still sent memos when the staples were not perfectly horizontal.

And then came the Internet.

Slowly at first, then faster, and now at breakneck pace, the ability to publish immediately to anyone, anywhere transformed the media as we knew it. If only the conventional media could work out how to really make money from it, we'd be laughing.

In pursuit of the science of reputation

What does all of this mean for public relations and its role in managing brand reputation? Long term, it is difficult, or impossible, to know precisely. A few things, though, are certain: getting to grips with a far more diverse media is a much more challenging job for PRs; influence must be managed at speed and media digitisation creates audit trails that will make the influencing of reputation more measurable.

Read that back again. First point: it's a far bigger job to get our heads around – so commercial wisdom is that automation is required. Second point: it moves faster – again, smells of automation. Third point: you can measure probable and absolute impact on reputation because of digitisation and, hence, automation.

So, as public relations enters a new age of sophistication and speed, is the art of public relations very much on the shelf as the whole thing becomes a science?

If you looked at the favoured talking points and daily brayings of the social media mob – those proponents of social media who seem to have the greatest self-interest in evangelising its merits for their own sake – you'd certainly be forgiven for thinking so. While some commentators using social media to spread information and their views focus on the changes happening in media overall, most narrow their gaze to social media, and in particular to the measurement of social media influence, social media sentiment, social media this and that. In fact, if social media broke wind they'd find a way to harness and analyse it.

That's harsh perhaps, but probably an inevitable situation, given that a massive scientific breakthrough – the Internet – made all of this change possible in the first place. The reality is that while media digitisation has created requirements and opportunities for public relations to become more scientific in its approach and its application, the human factor will of course always be at the heart of determining how content will best create publicity which influences reputation. We've had the appliance of science, now we have to apply the art part to a very different media landscape that continues to evolve.

The human beings in public relations have to use technological advances to gain a better understanding of their audiences and how their opinions change. They must use technology to find shrewder and more compelling ways to deliver their content. But most of all, they must understand how science is changing the media, and what demands the media now places on them as a professional. Because professional it has become. The public relations craftsman or woman who was largely focused on generating publicity in established media will not be replaced by a public relations scientist. It's not about art versus science. But modern PR people will have to take a smarter and harder-working approach to the art of editorial delivery, and have a real understanding of how the scientific stuff – such as the audience understanding, the monitoring of feedback and the measurement of results – works too.

The mere mention of science is enough to both bring a wry smile to the faces of long-in-the-tooth public relations practitioners and marketing directors keen to find any way to make the commercial value of public relations more tangible. While the value of public relations to many organisations is wholly recognised, it remains a dark art to some, and one that financiers have long wanted to model so that payback can be charted using mathematical formulae. Until now, regardless of the complexity of evaluation metrics used, while it has been possible to gauge at least some commercial perspective, it has been impossible to precisely measure the value of public relations on a unit cost basis by monetary means. And with the advent of editorial output that leaves an audit trail – in other words everything that has been published on the Internet – public relations measurement is becoming a whole lot more scientific.

Is a best-guess still best?

Before the Internet, or at least before social media and its ability to forge direct relationships with consumers, came along, PR's value and best-guess assumption were joined at the hip. Equally, the most severe outcomes of PR-influenced editorial – both good and bad – made measuring investment returns scientifically something of a fool's errand. If all the right press were writing all the right things about you and sales went up in the absence of much other marketing, then hey presto: good press means higher sales. If sales dipped when corporate reputation had taken a public beating, join the dots.

It'd be a bit like establishing monetary measurement for every last bit of legal advice a company is given for a court trial. Fundamentally, they know the advice has worked if they get the outcome they were seeking. But measuring the value of individual pieces of that advice would be more difficult, if not futile. And unlike public relations advice, legal advice can also give fast and direct payback, particularly where the outcome of proceedings is involved. Unlike legal advice, however, public relations has the ability to catapult a brand from obscurity or run-of-the-mill awareness to something that consumers just can't get enough of. It is the seismic effects of both public relations and routine editorial influence that keeps routine sales and customer retention ticking over nicely that brand owners would dearly love to get more scientific about.

Despite the technological advances that are revolutionising media, there remains no bulletproof model for accurately assessing how public relations investment generates a measurable impact on reputation. That is to say, there is no single model. There are many models that, when combined, can give a pretty scientific overview of reputation, and, therefore, the likelihood that a customer will buy a product or service, or even remain a customer. Ultimately though, the only way to gain true assurances over public relations spend and direct impact on reputation is to interrogate each customer at the point of purchase, or other key points during the customer lifecycle, and ask them telling questions about a brand's reputation. Even then, they might not answer the questions honestly.

Reputation, then, is a sod of a thing to measure. Many people have been well paid for trying to work out how best to measure it but have ultimately ended up with an interpretation of previous forms of measurement. Others have looked at all of those ways of trying to measure reputation and tried to piece them together, or stack them all up alongside each other, in order to draw conclusions. What they've drawn though, really, is a web of confusion.

In many ways, the Internet doesn't change that. In fact, think back to the last time you read a comment on a press article, on a blog post or on a Facebook update and tutted at the poor English used; you may have been left thinking that the Internet can make it even more difficult to assess the value of editorial influence on reputation simply because the audience can't spell very well, or does a good job of appearing incoherent. What the Internet does give us, and what social media experts therefore get very hot under the collar about, is an audit trail.

If a consumer is hacked off about something a brand has said or done, they can say so by typing their comments online, so that many other people – potentially millions of people – can see what they think. So the opinions that impact reputation can be measured. So too can the extent to which those opinions have been changed by editorial influence – both conventional and social media – online be measured. And public relations investment is fairly easy to measure, by counting what has been spent. Those correlations are clear, and the tools that enable these factors to be gauged and interpreted more usefully are becoming both simpler to use and more sophisticated by the day.

What cannot yet be measured, at least not in any clinical, scientific way, is the direct correlation between investment in specific public relations activities and overall brand reputation. You can measure an audience's opinion on a specific activity. You can measure, barometer-like, what the audience's view of the brand is and, therefore, the favourability of its reputation. But you cannot put both together and reach scientific conclusions.

So the quest for a public relations measurement model that enables every scrap of investment to be quantified against brand reputational change goes on. In the meantime, it doesn't really matter that much anyway, because there are far bigger matters at hand such as the impact of negative editorial on a brand's fortunes. When your reputation is being dumped on from a great height by a potent cross-section of consumers from across the world in a short space of time and sales dry up, more effective measurement of public relations investment is the last thing on your mind. Making it all stop is the priority.

Common sense and grown-up judgement prevail.

Judgement days

In fact, judgement has a lot to do with everything in this new media landscape. Brands are being judged like never before, and marketers are being asked to make judgement calls more quickly, and with the benefit of far less experience than ever before. The reason for this decision-making challenge is plain and simple: speed.

Think back to the days when all media was conventional media. What all major brands were looking for from public relations investment was word-of-mouth recommendation amongst their audiences. Sure, a brand can build reputation by gaining a public following through sustained editorial exposure. It can even do so relatively quickly. But nothing accelerates the fortunes of a brand quite like the effects of word-of-mouth. By causing human beings to converse about a brand or product amongst themselves, rather than just reading or hearing about it through the media, public relations can make or break a product's fortunes.

In today's world of social, owned and conventional media, the same is true. Only everything moves much, much faster. Word-of-mouth in the pub or park remains a potent factor. But online conversations have the advantage of being both preserved for eternity in digitised text and much easier to disseminate quickly amongst millions of people. Rather than relying on the same words being said in every park and pub up and down the land, just a few choice words circulated online can be pushed and pulled to the outer limits of social networks in minutes.

Judgement is, therefore, a highly prized thing. Make the right move and a brand can enjoy the glare of the attention of the online world, roused into conversation by a whirlwind knock-on effect. Get things wrong, and it can backfire catastrophically.

Social media has been a major change in the way that word-of-mouth impacts upon brand reputation. Again, speed is the driving force, but decisions about what brands should say, and how they should behave, have the greatest bearing on how a brand fares. Yet there are two big problems in making those decisions: the organisational structure that all too often does not allow sound decisions to be made quickly enough, and the cultural adjustment needed to a media that cannot be controlled – partly because of the pace at which it moves, and partly because of the sheer scale and scope of the conversations that it hosts. It can be like all of your worst enemies deciding to get together and talk venomously about you, while all of your best friends are listening. Not comfortable territory.

Word-of-mouth, then, is the most powerful asset that public relations has at its disposal. Editorial influence is critical too, but its ability to trigger talk purely because the right things are said or done is what sets it apart from other types of marketing. With that power, though, comes a new kind of responsibility and an appreciation that both listening to and understanding the audience intimately is needed if a right royal cockup is to be avoided.

The judgement required isn't actually that difficult. It is mostly rooted in common sense, albeit needing large amounts of editorial skill, audience understanding and media insight to be effective. The problem is that all too often, politics and organisational pressures stand firmly in the way of common sense.

Of course, every brand has its own unique challenges. Yet there are a bunch of fundamentals that are a given. They are rules that, if you think about it, apply equally to all conversations where the people you're talking to are people you know and understand, and where others may end up joining the conversation during its course.

First, know who you're talking to. Not just *who* they are, but what their views are on the things you'll be talking about and, given their attitudes and behaviour (all of which can be comprehensively assessed if they're active on social media platforms), what their views on other things are likely to be.

Then you need to think about what point you're trying to get across. It may well be a wholly self-serving thing about your brand. But if you're not focused on it, it will soon drift into waffle.

Finally, you need to be alert to the change in conversational tone, direction and opinion that can be driven by group dynamics. Just as in real word-of-mouth scenarios, as one person receives a message and then passes it on for others to hear, brands must be alive to how the content evolves and how it may need to change what it says as a result.

Simple? It can be. Yet the discomfort that is caused by lack of overall control still strikes fear into the hearts of brands. Often, it is not in their nature: many brands are set up to try to deliver influence and manage reputation through conventional media as it operated in the past. Today, reputations can shift quickly because influence can take hold in minutes, not in weeks or months. The old media conventions of 'deadline week' for a monthly magazines, 'deadline day' for a weekly title and a series of deadlines throughout the morning or evening for a daily newspaper have been swept aside by what the Internet has done for publishing.

Today, deadlines are more important than ever, yet equally there is often no deadline at all because the deadline is simply as soon as you can type your opinion and press 'send'.

Gaining command, not seizing control

So if you're a brand, it's time to open your eyes. Not to the realisation that social media is quite cool because it allows a different kind of brand influence to be created. Not because changing media is changing the management of reputation. And not because the Internet has created online conversational media that can fuel new levels of reputational impact through word-of-mouth techniques.

The eyes of brands need to be open to *all* of these things. Brands need to harness media change rather than stepping back and scratching their heads. They need to work out where control can be gained, rather than staring at social media like a rabbit in the headlights. They need to look at how they manage communication, and roles and responsibilities, and at how audiences are reacting to it around the clock.

And they need to look at their own people, right the way to the top. Take one look at the brands that are most highly prized in the world today and it's not hard to see that the enigmatic executives that lead those organisations play a central role in their reputations. Often, everything they do or say in public, whether in front of a microphone, typed online or spoken into a video camera, will be pored over by watching commentators, not least the conventional media.

Today's CEOs don't just run the company, they run 'the show'. The brand's show. Its 'public performance'. The central thread of its reputation.

In years gone by, chief executives and managing directors could operate below the radar in a public sense, with few people amongst their external audiences perhaps even knowing their name. That is beginning to change. Of course, the technology companies in Silicon Valley and the Internet mega-entrepreneurs have led the way, but think about airlines, oil and gas companies, major retailers and clothing brands and the average person can surely name far more of their chief executives than they could a decade ago. The fragmentation, immediacy, and personal and viral nature of modern media has not just put the CEO in the spotlight, it has often put the spotlight in the hands of the audience.

Today's senior executives don't just need to be comfortable in front of the media – adept at giving quotes and working the editorial process in press interviews, likeable and believable on TV, compelling on radio and so on – they need to be comfortable in front of the world. They need to focus on body language and vocal inflection as in days gone by, but it's the words that now count more than ever. Those words can have greater power over reputation because of their reach and their immediacy. Equally, they can have a greater negative impact too.

For this reason, some brands front other senior executives alongside, or instead of, the person at the very top. Media-wise, it means you can cover more ground. You can do more to show you understand your customers and your people. You can compensate for any lack of natural media ability in the person at the helm. Given the volume of media now at brands' disposal, spokespeople could come from anywhere within the organisation, and beyond it within the customer base – not as official spokespeople, but as important advocates.

The spotlight has never been more intense. But just because you think you have more to say and you have more credible, expert and empathetic people to do the talking doesn't mean that you're necessarily going to get an easier ride. Just because you have strength in depth doesn't mean that you can gain a tighter grip on your reputation.

For one simple reason: it's just not possible.

The best way to look at it is that your brand cannot gain control, but it can gain, or take, command. But only if it understands the media and audience intimately, and so plots the right content. That, of course, is just the opening gambit of the conversation, and the brand must be ready to engage in fruitful dialogue rather than hiding under skirts when tongues get rough. But with clear insight, considered wisdom, sound ability to execute and an unhindered view of the desired outcome, brands have so much to gain.

This is because they can command conversations, command editorial attention and so command the respect that builds reputation. As Mike Walsh says, 'There is an urgent need to define transparency. Organisations try to control it, but they must face the facts. It is uncontrollable.'

Reputation is the result of what you do, what you say and what people therefore think and say about you. The digitisation of media can put you in greater command of it. But you must know the game, and play it right.

'Brands aren't all yours, anyway'

Mike Walsh has witnessed more advertising campaigns for more brands than you've had hot dinners. The former European chief executive of Ogilvy began his career in advertising in the early 1970s and has represented clients like Air Canada, American Express, Beecham Foods, Polaroid and Spillers Petfoods.

For him, today's frenetic media change brings with it a need for communicators to keep cool heads. As he sees it, there is a need for business leaders to rise above the noise that is associated with digital media and marketing change to remember one of the fundamental truths: that brands are created by consumers and exist in their minds.

So the organisations that own the brands cannot control the brands – because they are partly the 'property' of the consumers or audiences that are on the outside looking in. Equally, brand managers should not be singularly focused on structural or organisational changes that they make to their marketing teams and programmes to address modern media, as to do so means they're focusing on themselves rather than establishing how they can best use new media to forge stronger brand perception and desire amongst their audiences.

'Brands need to think about attitude change, not organisational change,' says Walsh. 'Digital media, and in particular the capacity for media to be mobile, right in the pockets of consumers, presents a huge opportunity for them to redefine transparency. The problem is that organisations try to control this; they try to control the media content that has a bearing on how they will be perceived, but it is fundamentally uncontrollable. While it is a major and uncomfortable change for most brands, they are having to become far more transparent, and build credibility and integrity through the ways in which they engage with consumers directly and engage with the media to drive editorial.'

Yet organisational change is required if brands are to be more effective at managing their reputations, readying themselves to reduce the impact of reputational damage and meeting the expectations of audiences that can now engage with them directly. For Walsh, this can only start at the top, but who the people are, how they behave and how they're perceived has an increasing effect on overall brand reputation. And there is absolutely no way to hide from that.

'The people in organisations are increasingly important. One third of the overall shareholder value comes from the chief executive officer, and specifically it comes from their reputation. That is clearly an enormous part of the value of the business, and editorial in its broadest, most modern and rapidly changing sense has to be utilised to the full to help build and maintain that value,' he says.

But the person in the hot seat cannot do it alone. There is too much media, there are too many other demands on their time, and the pace at which brand narratives – or other stories that are completely beyond their control – develop is such that resources required to develop and manage the communication must be expansive, agile and well-marshalled.

'Managing the reputation of the CEO is one of the biggest tasks that public relations now faces. Their personal life is now transparent too. Public relations agencies should be looking to step forward and play the part of custodian in all of this, as chief executives clearly need a lot of help to get it right. The relatively high turnover of CEOs as a result of damaged reputations, for example, when energy firms have mishandled communication around oil spills, is such that someone needs to be asking why it is that they get it so wrong,' says Walsh.

Summary

- In the past, many brands may have felt they had a degree of control over what was written and said about them in the established press. They were never really in control, yet influence was typically a simpler thing to come by.
- The ability to influence brand reputation through modern, digitised media may seem fairly fragile, but corporate communicators need to put themselves on firmer foundations.
- The editorial world is continuing to change rapidly, meaning the techniques for influencing editorial are changing too.
- Pioneers in the reputation game pursued early scientific approaches to creating and sustaining influence. We can learn something from this today.

- Brands are more in the spotlight than ever because modern media makes them more accessible. It is easy for them to be judged by the public.
- It's about taking steps to gaining command of reputation and how it influences, because seizing control is impossible.
- CEOs are much more in the spotlight, and brands need to scrutinise how best to handle that.
- Brands aren't all yours anyway: they exist in the minds of consumers, and public relations professionals would do well to remember that.

CHAPTER

2

MEDIA: TRADITIONAL VERSUS DIGITAL

The Internet has destroyed every business model that it has touched. The media industry continues to rebuild its future. #brandanarchy

It's almost certainly too early to predict what the future of the traditional media industry will look like. One thing is for sure though; it cannot continue without radical transformation. Greg Dyke was chief executive of London Weekend Television, now part of ITV, in the early 1990s. He learnt the hard way the folly of ignoring technological disruption in the media business. His lesson for the current generation of media entrepreneurs could not be clearer. 'We made good programmes and had a good, profitable business. Then along came Sky and multi-channel television and pay television. We pretended it wasn't happening, just as the music industry has over the last 10 years. Instead of embracing the new world ourselves and sacrificing some of our current profits, we thought that we could see it off,' said Dyke. Two decades later, ITV is rebuilding itself again around a fragmented media proposition. Ignoring the emergence of multi-channel television was a harsh lesson.

The decline of print

Today, newsprint continues to have huge authority in the UK. Brands such as the *Daily Mirror* (founded 1903), *Financial Times* (founded 1888), *Sunday Times* (founded 1821) and *Wall Street Journal* (founded 1889) have delivered the news to us each day for more than a century. They are a cornerstone of the media establishment. An online news site, often with a history of no more than a decade, always takes second place to a print article in terms of authority, however relevant to its audience. Even a story in the *FT* or *WSJ* has greater social creditability than anything in their online counterparts (FT.com[1] or WSJ.com[2]). It's a generational issue but it's also reality. But the situation is changing, and fast. People are reading online content more widely than ever before because they can access more information, more quickly, which indicates that they almost certainly do not have the time to spend reading a newspaper. Welcome to the era of snack media.

The 1980s and 1990s were the golden era of newsprint. *The Times* newspaper used to sell 820,000 copies per day (1997) and *The Sun* almost 4.8 million copies per day (1987). Now it's 500,000 and three million respectively. Each month in the UK, the Audit Bureau of Circulations (ABC)[3] plots the decline in newsprint readership and the corresponding increase in the web audience for online news. The audience for newsprint is in free fall, and ageing. You could predict the date that the last newspaper will be printed by using annuity tables. Broadsheet and tabloid audiences are declining by an average of 10 per cent per year. Print won't die anytime soon but its decline is irreversible and there will almost certainly be fewer print products by 2020. Whenever we talk to groups of journalists or communications professionals we ask for a show of hands from anyone who has bought a copy of a national newspaper that day. Only a few hands ever go up. If people in the media and public relations industries aren't buying newspapers, what hope is there for the industry? It's a rhetorical question.

---

1 FT.com: www.ft.com/home/uk
2 WSJ.com: europe.wsj.com
3 Audit Bureau of Circulations (ABC) www.abc.org.uk

The primary function of newspapers is to service an audience once a day. Huge investment has been made in paper, printing and distribution to deliver a product to your doorstep. Yet via your Internet connection you can access every single news publisher that you could possibly want, whenever you want, and as often as you want. In this sense, the conventional media industry's monopoly on news has been destroyed by the Internet. The well-established media brands that have dominated the business of news for so long must now compete for our attention along with the thousands of outlets on the Internet. It is little wonder that newsprint struggles to make money when it faces such stiff competition for our attention from millions of online publications, blogs and social media websites. No longer does the news business reside with a handful of terrestrial television channels and a small number of newspaper publishers. It's plain old economics. When supply in a market is restricted it is possible for a small number of operators to build highly profitable businesses. But remove all barriers, as the Internet has with the news business, and the market becomes much more to make money.

There is plenty of evidence to support the decline of newsprint but our appetite for media content appears insatiable. According to OFCOM's 2010 Communication Market Report[4], people in the UK spend about seven hours a day consuming different media but they consume more and more during this time by so-called media multitasking. A fifth of this time is spent using more than one form of media simultaneously. This results in people squeezing almost nine hours of media consumption into

---

4   2010 Communication Market Report, OFCOM: http://stakeholders.ofcom.
    org.uk/market-data-research/market-data/communications-market-
    reports/cmr10/

seven hours. More specifically, the number of hours that 16 to 24-year-olds spend consuming media is lower than in older age groups, but 29 per cent of their time is spent using several media forms concurrently, meaning that they fit nine hours and 32 minutes' worth of media consumption into every day. You need look no further than your living room for evidence. When families or groups of friends sits down to watch television they are increasingly using Facebook or Twitter on laptops or mobile phones to engage in conversations with friends who are watching TV elsewhere. This is the future of media, and it's participatory.

Broadcast is booming

Print may be in trouble but broadcast media is booming. Digital broadcasting disconnects television from the programme schedules and means that content can be viewed on demand. Furthermore, technical developments such as 3D and high definition (HD) are driving growth for content that makes use of these new formats and broadens the appeal of television for consumers. That said, we don't think we'll see the death of the television schedule anytime soon. Open Twitter during a popular current affairs programme or the networked television programme and you'll discover the reason why. During 2011, the BBC started to include hashtags within television programmes so that viewers could participate in the programme via Twitter. Hashtags are descriptive tags appended with a # such as #bbcqt (comment on the BBC Question Time TV programme) or #London (content about London) that enable topics such be searched within a stream of social media content. Without doubt, television has wholeheartedly embraced the social media concept: 'Television is fundamentally a social media experience. It generates content that is shared and discussed on platforms such as Facebook and Twitter,' says

Howard Kosky, managing director of broadcast public relations agency markettiers4dc[5].

Radio listening in the UK, like television watching, is close to saturation with 91.6 per cent of the UK population tuning in to the radio each week, according to radio tracking data published by RAJAR[6]. Listening to radio via a digital platform has risen by more than 10 per cent year-on-year from 2010 to 2011, with 19.7 million people tuning in to radio via a digitally-enabled set each week. Radio, too, is becoming social. Arguably it always has been, with radio phone-ins being a staple of many programmes, but in more recent times, helped by Apple's iTunes platform, radio has given rise to a new genre of audio called the podcast. This enables anybody to create and circulate audio content using a PC or mobile device such as a smartphone. 'The popularity of broadcast is down to three factors; access, availability and brand. You can listen to the radio or watch television on your computer, mobile phone or MP3 player either live in real time or on demand, and broadcast brands have strong well-defined personalities,' says Kosky.

Changing media habits

You can plot the demise of print through the generations. We have observed it first hand in our own families. Stephen's grandfather receives both a morning and an evening newspaper, as he has for the 40 years that I have been alive. The *Daily Telegraph* or *The Guardian* in the morning; chosen not because of any political leaning but because of the crosswords; and the regional evening paper for local news. He is almost certainly

---

5 Markettiers4dc: www.markettiers4dc.com
6 Data Release – Quarter 1, 2011, RAJAR: www.rajar.co.uk/docs/news/data_release_2011_Q1.pdf

one of the very few in the UK who subscribe to both a daily morning and evening paper. Our parents' generation haven't the time to read both a morning and an evening paper, while members of our generation are unlikely to read a newspaper unless they live in a city where the *Metro* is circulated for free. Our children, by contrast, are unlikely to ever subscribe to a daily newspaper. It's far more likely that they'll get their local news from their Facebook newsfeed.

According to Francis Ingham, director general of the Public Relations Consultants Association (PRCA)[7] in the UK, the very fact that media as we knew it has changed so quickly has caught both communications people and brands on the hop. 'One of the main difficulties the public relations industry faces in modernising is that we have got used to communicating mainly via print and have been doing it for so long. People are now bombarded with more and more news,' he says. He believes that in the future, media will have to become more specialised. A mass of niche audience publications, or information services, will ensure that editorial is punchy and individualised, to overcome the glut of mainstream news options that are currently available. 'The future of the media will undoubtedly see fewer newspapers being read by fewer people. And the footprint of online newspapers will diminish because of paywalls that block access to a website unless a payment is made. Our reckoning is that we will see more editorial outlets and they will be read by more people. Yet we do delude ourselves into thinking there was a golden era of journalism, which just isn't the case. Publishing has all too frequently been a vanity exercise, and few people have really been able to make good money from conventional publishing alone,' he adds.

---

7   Public Relations Consultants Association (PRCA): www.prca.org.uk

The new media

David Phillips, a public relations practitioner and academic, is co-author with Phillip Young of Online Public Relations[8]. He believes that social media is a natural evolution of human development and rooted in our psyche. 'The leap from throwing a spear to inventing a bow and arrow was huge. But using technology you can shoot a spear much further. You can run fast but on a bike you can go further. You can remember lots of text but if you have access to Google you can remember everything. We are extending our physiology. If you go back to the Internet when it first started, it was a technology-driven thing for technologists so that they could be better at what they did'.

In time, we'll come to recognise the development of Internet technologies at the turn of the 21st century to be as radical to society as the invention of the printing press was in the second half of the 15th century. The printing press meant that pamphlets, newspapers and books could be printed in large numbers and distributed. It was an expensive process but it removed the limitations of manual copying. Developments in Internet publishing applications mean that anyone with a web browser and an Internet connection can become an online publisher.

Services such as Blogger[9] from Pyro Labs (launched in 1999 and purchased by Google in 2003), TypePad[10] (launched 2003) and Wordpress[11] (launched 2003) allow content to be published on the Internet in a blog format. Blogs are usually maintained by an individual with content published in date order. Most are interactive, allowing visitors to interact with the publisher or

---

8 Phillips, David, and Young, Philip. *Online Public Relations*. Kogan Page, 2009.
9 Blogger: www.blogger.com
10 TypePad: www.typepad.com
11 Wordpress: wordpress.org

blogger via comments. Initially blogs were used by motivated individuals to publish their comments or opinions but quickly became recognised as a means for individuals to engage directly with an audience. By 2004, blogging had started to become a mainstream communications activity. Politicians, business professionals and journalists started to use blogs as a means of communicating their expertise. According to Nielsen's BlogPulse[12], there are now more than 156 million public blogs in existence. The launch of the social networking site Twitter in 2006 gave blogging a shot in the arm. It enabled bloggers to post and share their content and invite comment directly from followers.

Head to Google Blog Search[13] or Technorati[14], the user-generated media search engine, or a commercial tool such as BlogPulse, and search on a topic. You'll find hundreds of blogs returned, whatever your area of interest. If you don't, congratulations: you have found one of the few topic areas that is poorly served by blogs. We suggest that you start blogging immediately.

One of the strongest topics for blogging is parenting. It is easy to understand why. New parents, typically mums, head to the web to find out information about being a new parent, to reach out to people in a similar situation and share their views. Parenting blogs started initially as a medium for journalists and marketing people on maternity leave. But the sector has developed to embrace lawyers, doctors, schoolteachers, and stay-at-home mums.

According to Sally Whittle, founder of TOTS 100[15] a community of more than 1,000 parenting blogs, blogging is booming with

---

12 BlogPulse: www.blogpulse.com
13 Google Blog Search: www.google.com/blogsearch
14 Technorati: technorati.com
15 TOTS 100: www.tots100.co.uk

mums and dads joining in greater numbers. 'They come from all walks of life and experiences. It's mainly mums, although not exclusively, who blog as a means of sharing ideas and building a network,' says Whittle. Blogging mums are a hugely influential audience in the fragmented media landscape for any organisation that is seeking to reach and engage new parents or families. Consumer brands and even politicians recognised the opportunity to connect with an influencial audience. Whittle sells access to her TOTS100 community to organisations and public relations firms that wish to connect with bloggers.

The June 2011 CyberMummy Conference[16] in London attracted more than 30 sponsors including Boots, Butlins, Disney, Hewlett-Packard and Procter & Gamble, all keen to connect with the 400 bloggers that attended the event. In the lead-up to the 2010 UK general election, each of the party leaders took part in a web chat on Mumsnet[17], the UK community website set up to allow parents to share views and advice on parenting and family issues. The benefit of engaging with an audience via a blog or community website is the transparency and direct participatory connection that it provides.

The public relations industry has been quick to spot the potential for blogs to connect their clients with target audiences but often with limited success. The public relations industry is a broad church and is itself going through rapid change as it modernises. Some practitioners are excellent at blogger relations; some are still learning. Practitioners have used the media relations skills that they have developed to pitch content to journalists, to work with bloggers and have expected them to be directly transferable. They aren't. There are similarities but

16 CyberMummy Conference: www.cybermummy.com
17 Mumsnet: www.mumsnet.com

the motivations of a blogger are very different from those of a journalist. Bloggers typically fit writing around a full-time career or and are motivated by their own interests.

The best way to understand a parenting blogger is to follow their blog and to meet them face-to-face if you get the chance. If you want to learn about working with bloggers, there is no better way than attending blogging events such as the CyberMummy Conference. Below are some tips from a bloggers versus public relations industry debate at a bloggers' meet-up[18] in London.

Successful blogger relations

Databases of blogs are the enemy of good public relations and blogger relationships. PRs should plan campaigns by understanding the blogs that they are targeting and not spamming an email list.

Relevancy, relationships and respect are the key to successful blogger relations. Abuse of these fundamental tenets of public relations has been an issue for the industry for the last 30 years.

If you're planning to run a sponsored blogging programme, do it transparently. All bloggers targeted as part of a campaign should be treated equally.

Bloggers may expect to be sponsored to participate in an event, write or comment about a client, just as PRs are paid by their clients to pitch stories.

There is no better way of gaining experience of blogger relations than to start blogging yourself.

---

18 Commonsense prevails at bloggers vs PRs meetup:
www.speedcommunications.com/blogs/wadds/2010/09/09/
commonsense-prevails-at-pr-vs-bloggers-meetup

Journalism versus user-generated content

In debates about the future of media, the future of journalism and the future of publishing are almost always incorrectly interchanged. But journalism isn't a business model. It is a professional activity by which information and knowledge is gathered and conveyed to an audience. Proponents of digital media have called time on the mainstream media and claim that blogs, Facebook, Google + and Twitter are the new currency for news for most consumers. There is no doubt that news travels fast via trusted contacts through networks such as Twitter and that so-called 'citizen journalists', armed with no more than a camera phone, can share images from the location of a news event before professional journalists can reach the scene. But for every example of citizen journalism that has broken a story, there are countless examples of social media being used to push propaganda or news stories that are plainly incorrect.

Social media may have a role within news reporting but it needs to be treated with the same level of deference as any other source. Stories can spread incredibly quickly in social media, a characteristic that organisations work hard to mimic. Agencies and brands carefully craft content with the goal of inspiring like-minded consumers to forward it through their networks. Armies of communication professionals are creating content with the goal of baiting people to circulate it in networks.

'Viral' is the term used to describe this mechanism. Much has been written about how you create viral content, but in truth it is impossible to guarantee how a network will respond to content. There are simply too many variables to predict any given outcomes. Creating content that goes viral is the ultimate goal of any Internet marketing professional. How often have you forwarded a link via Twitter or clicked your mouse over a 'like' button on Facebook without checking on the authenticity or even the accuracy of the content? The tools that make it easy to create and publish content to build reputation can just as easily be used for malicious or ill-informed intent. It is all too easy to create official looking accounts on social networks such as Twitter and Facebook which contain erroneous content that would fool most consumers.

Asda, the UK supermarket owned by Walmart, experienced this issue at first hand in June 2011. Back in 2008, an Asda advertisement for DVDs, aimed at fathers, was placed in the *Daily Mirror* alongside a news story about wife-beating. It was plainly inappropriate and was the result of poor layout on the part of newspaper. On a typical day, there are approximately 1,000 posts on Twitter about Asda. That rose to 6,000 as the dodgy *Daily Mirror* page layout was circulated by Twitter users in June 2011 with the intent of embarrassing Asda. The fact that content was, by that time, several years old didn't occur to the people circulating a link to the content. They clearly weren't *Daily Mirror* readers, and they didn't check the original source of the content, otherwise they would have realised their error.

Asda head of corporate communications, Dominic Burch, suspected foul play on the part of a detractor stoking up an old story. 'We were first made aware of the issue by an agency that works for Asda which spotted the story being circulated by email. That was Tuesday. By Friday there were 2,000 tweets per day. By Saturday that number rose to 6,000,' says Burch. The Asda communications teams decided not to respond proactively to the issue, deciding that its impact on the supermarket's reputation was marginal. 'We took the view that despite all the noise on Twitter it was fairly harmless in the scheme of things. It was clearly a bit dated, using our old brand, promoting old movies and out-of-date pricing. The inappropriate layout clearly resulted from the *Daily Mirror*'s production rather than Asda choosing to be on that page by that article. After seeing the umpteenth tweet we started to respond directly to people, particularly those who should know better than to repeat a tweet without verifying first, asking them to check that day's newspaper,' says Burch.

But the content appeared sufficiently authentic to be circulated by consumers. The fact that the advertisement was a Father's Day promotion from several years before and that all of the DVDs were clearly out of date was clearly irrelevant. If a newspaper publishes content that is erroneous, there is a clear process for retribution – usually an apology. But in social media, no such rules apply. Asda would need to prove defamation before it could seek redress from the Facebook or Twitter users that circulated the dodgy content.

There are two postscripts to this story that prove that Burch and his team made the right call. Journalists from national newspapers picked up the story from their own Twitter accounts and called Asda directly asking for comment. In each case they were told that if they checked the *Daily Mirror*, they would find that the offending layout was several years old. No one in the conventional media thought the story worthy of an article except the diary page of *The Grocer*, which later published an apology and a letter from Burch. Finally, when in-store sales receipts for DVDs the week following the event were assessed, they showed a significant rise during the weekend that the *Daily Mirror* layout gaffe was doing the rounds on Facebook and Twitter. The team's quick reaction ensured not only that the situation didn't develop into a crisis but that it also helped to drive sales.

Maintaining standards

There can be no doubt that individuals are supplementing the work of journalists in providing content from news events via networks such as Facebook, Flickr, Twitter and YouTube, often long before journalists get to the story. That's because anyone equipped with a mobile device is now prospectively a multimedia journalist. Following the earthquake in Haiti in 2010, the first images out of the country came via Flickr and the first source of information about actual conditions on the ground was a social media wiki site that enabled anyone to add, delete or revise content. Members of social networking sites such as Facebook and Twitter spread messages to help kick-start the fundraising effort.

But social media has a role to play in professional journalism. It is enabling journalists to innovate when and how they pull together stories. You can see this played out every single day on websites as stories are developed and managed by journalists. News organisations such as the Associated Press and the BBC have recruited social media specialists to scrutinise and check content from user-generated sources and networks such as Facebook and Twitter. There can be no doubt that individuals have a role to play in breaking news stories but as a minimum, journalists need to make contact with the source and take steps to verify content, as they should for any story. The news business might be in a state of flux, but the basic tenets of professional journalism must be maintained.

There's a very real danger as production budgets for news organisations come under increasing pressure for publishers to cut costs. The demise of the subeditor is one of the tragedies of the shift from print to online news publishing. Once upon a time, a sub would act as gatekeeper of quality, correcting and tightening up copy before a journalist submitted it for page layout. But that role is disappearing fast as budgets are reduced, and increasingly, journalists file copy direct to a production environment or a live website without review. The result is an inevitable drop in standards.

Changing media models

In contrast to the decline in print circulation, online newspaper audiences are growing steadily, albeit in an increasingly competitive environment for news. But the notion that a company can charge a premium for a media product that is 24 hours out of date when it hits the newsstand, yet gives away its content for free throughout the day, is an anachronism. There has been a brutal awakening in the newspaper industry that advertising revenues are never going to make up for the shortfall in revenue following the shift from print to online.

The story of the decline in newsprint first began in the mid-1990s when Internet dial-up access became a mainstream consumer product. Entrepreneurs spotted the opportunity for disruptive business models that were able to take advertising revenue away from the newspaper industry. The newsprint industry's losses have been the gain of businesses such as Craigslist, eBay and Google, which attracted advertisers by creating online businesses that were able to match buyer and seller more efficiently than print.

The game was up for newsprint long before Apple launched the iPad and Amazon launched the Kindle. Other manufacturers followed suit with a variety of tablet devices. But perhaps the emerging market in newspaper applications – 'apps' – for mobile devices points to a potential future where consumers may be willing to pay for digital news content as consumers pay for content in this new format. The iPad recreates the immersive environment and production qualities of a newspaper. Content follows a standard format and layout driven by production values. The reader follows a path through the newspaper set out by the editorial team rather than the click-and-mix approach of a website.

Online newspaper audiences are growing steadily thanks to a combination of apps and the web. If the print media is to have any future as a sustainable business, the shortfall in income between circulation, advertising and product costs must be addressed. If companies can't make the news business pay, then perhaps one potential future for the news industry lies in ownership by a single wealthy individual. *The Independent* and the London *Evening Standard* are both owned by Russian billionaire Alexander Lebedev, and Richard Desmond owns *The Daily Express*. We're living through a period of intense innovation in the media industry. Each national newspaper is developing its own very different business models online. It's early days as publishers seek to build sustainable models.

What will readers pay for?

The *Financial Times* has an enviable position as a media property with unique content and a point of view for which customers are willing to pay. It has implemented a combination of models. A standard subscription at £3.79 per week buys unlimited access to the FT.com website, mobile phone and iPad versions, and a five-year company financial archive. An extra £1.70 per week buys the LEX column and access to it in an electronic format. The FT has also implemented micropayments. If you're not a regular FT.com reader you can view 10 articles for free per month before you have to buy a day pass or pay-per-view.

It is not possible to discuss the future of the news business without a mention of Rupert Murdoch and News Corporation. Murdoch has built his empire around the news business, initially in print, and latterly in television broadcast media. He's arguably one of the last defenders of print. His forays into social media have not been successful, although he appears to be staking the future of his organisation on paywalls and apps. *The Times* and the *Sunday Times*, both owned by News Corporation, have led the way in the UK with paywalls. The content went behind a paywall in July 2010 when a 24-hour day pass was priced at £1 and weekly access at £2. It claims 105,000 total transactions for digital content between July and October 2010, of which half were one-offs, meaning the number of repeat subscribers is around 50,000 split across the web, iPad and Kindle.

In tabloid land, the *Daily Mail* is the only UK daily newspaper with a clear strategy for generating revenue from its Mail Online service. Its approach is focused on generating potent content to bait traffic and appeal to advertisers. It's easy to see how it is done. The right-hand side of the homepage is packed with news stories optimised for search engine traffic more typical of the red top tabloid or weekly gossip magazines. Add to this the willingness on the part of the *Daily Mail* to embrace social media. At least 10 per cent of its traffic is reported to come from Facebook[19]. This strategy of appealing to a mass audience is clearly working; the question is whether this approach is scalable as it targets the US market in a bid to build a larger audience.

The *Daily Telegraph*'s web strategy is the most inventive of all the newspaper publishers. It is focused on the so-called three Cs: content, commerce and communities. At its most crude, the *Daily Telegraph* model uses editorial content to generate commerce around special interest communities. The *Daily Telegraph* Fashion Channel[20] matches digital editorial content with clothes shopping options via affiliate partners. It is following a print model of publishing daily at 5 a.m. rather than the web model of constantly updating content throughout the day.

---

19 Facebook generates 10 per cent of Mail Online's UK traffic, *The Guardian*:
  www.guardian.co.uk/media/2010/nov/15/mail-online-uk-traffic-facebook
20 The Telegraph Fashion: fashion.telegraph.co.uk/

The Guardian is backing a so-called 'digital first' strategy after making operating losses of £33 million in 2010. That hasn't resulted in the closure of the newspaper but it will see the paper invest heavily in its digital content. Like the *Daily Mail*, it opened a New York office in 2011 and has the US market in its sights, with a potential audience of almost 310 million versus its domestic UK market, which is a fifth of that size.

No limits content

The web removes the restrictions on a news organisation of page count and deadline. When a journalist is filing content to a web server rather than a print publication, page count and print deadlines are irrelevant. This has enabled newspapers to follow stories as they develop in real time and to publish live content, often in the form of blogs or real-time news feeds. Some publications such as *The Guardian* and the *Daily Telegraph* create microsites for big news stories which combine text, audio and video. This puts publishers in competition with broadcasters and social media channels to be the first to break and update news stories, but this is not an entirely healthy state of affairs.

In 2010, a major police operation took place in the north east of England when Raoul Moat, a 37-year-old man, went on the run after shooting three people, one of whom died. Moat headed to the village of Rothbury in Northumberland. During the ensuing six days of the search for him, Rothbury, a small town of 1,700 people, become a centre for the UK's media as radio, TV and print outlets set up camp. Rothbury residents were polarised in their response to the manhunt, choosing either to stay indoors or go about their lives as normal. Those who did venture out were sought out by journalists to comment on the story. Social networks such as Facebook and Twitter spawned discussions as the search for Moat progressed. Every aspect of the story was debated and discussed online. BBC News and Sky

News focused its coverage on the live story. This technique, known as 'monstering', is increasingly used by rolling news outlets when a big story breaks. Journalists used Twitter to communicate with each other and their audience, thereby crossing a line, possibly for the first time on a major news story, between personal comment, speculation and reporting.

The police tracked down Moat on the sixth day of the investigation and were involved in a standoff on a river bank in Rothbury. Journalists recognised that the story was reaching a conclusion but were thwarted when Northumbria Police took the unusual step[21] of directly asking the media to back off, via Twitter and other media, and put in place a 10-mile exclusion zone claiming that media presence was affecting the ongoing operation. Moat shot himself in the early hours of the following morning and was later pronounced dead at Newcastle General Hospital.

But the story didn't end at this point. User-generated eye witness video footage showing the eventual standoff between Moat and the police was published by the BBC[22] and a Moat tribute page on Facebook spawned 17,000 fans before it was removed on the grounds of decency by Facebook. The media's handling of big news stories has often courted controversy and stimulated debate. But the real-time nature of the Internet amplifies discussion and democratises communication so that everyone has an equal voice, meaning that a more stringent editorial function is arguably more important than ever.

---

21 Twitter message issued by Northumbria Police (@NorthumbriaPol): http://
    twitter.com/#!/NorthumbriaPol/status/18144945760
22 Gunman Raoul Moat's final stand-off caught on film, BBC News: www.bbc.
    co.uk/news/10593907

'Google charged'

Google is frequently charged with nicking the classified income from print newspapers and stealing the eyeballs of readers. Google aggressively counters the claim that it is a parasite feeding off conventional media, citing the four to five billion clicks a month that it sends to online news websites. The real issue is that the saturated. Paywalls help newspapers overcome this issue but in doing so they shrink the audience that is willing to pay to access content as customers that have traditionally been able to access content for free are expected to pay for access. A similar charge is frequently levelled at the BBC. In his 2009 speech to the Edinburgh Television Festival, James Murdoch accused the BBC of dumping state-funded news content on the Internet. The theory is that if we're not willing to pay, we can head to BBC News Online, or Google will efficiently find us another source.

The news industry has a feisty relationship with Google. But it only has itself to blame. In July 2011, Copiepresse, a Belgian copyright management company, pursued a claim against Google for including excerpts of its content in Google News search results[23]. A court ordered that Google must pay a licence fee or face penalties. Google's response was to remove newspapers that were members of Copiepresse from its search results, much to their irritation.

Who are the new newsagents?

Owning the relationship with the consumer is the big game to play for in the media and technology industries. With it, supply chains and markets that have existed for more than a century

---

23 Google blocks Belgian newspapers from web searches, MSN: www.msnbc. msn.com/id/43775017/ns/technology_and_science-tech_and_gadgets/t/ google-blocks-belgian-newspapers-web-searches/

in print publishing — and more recently in gaming, music and video distribution — are up for grabs. The race is on to create the new global entertainment store. 'Media disintegration' is an oft-used phrase but it lies at the heart of these market shifts. The web has democratised the market for content publishing, enabling anyone to reach a global audience at a low cost.

Consumers' demands are straightforward. They want access to content on their device of choice, in a seamless way. It's no longer good enough for a technology manufacturer to deliver hardware alone. Instead, they must create appealing hardware but also the infrastructure and services to deliver content. It's a very different way to how technology companies have operated in the past, but it gives them a shot at getting higher up the food chain and, crucially, a means of dramatically improving margins.

Predictions for growth of this new media infrastructure are dazzling. They differ wildly from market analyst to market analyst, perhaps because no one can get their head around the scale of the opportunity. Apple created has created its own flavour of hardware in the form of the iPhone and iPad, and the iTunes market was developed for software developers and publishers to sell their applications and content. The sacrifice that companies wanting to sell their wares in that market must make is to hand over 30 per cent of revenues to Apple, the cut it demands to distribute content via iTunes. Inevitably, publishers that have been used to managing their own supply chain aren't impressed with this model, particularly given that Apple owns the relationship with the consumer and as a result audience data. Google is alone in creating an open standard called Android. It has its own hardware platform thanks to the acquisition of Motorola's mobile telecommunications business[24]

24 Google to Acquire Motorola Mobility, Google Press release: http://investor. google.com/releases/2011/0815.html

and to collaboration with third-party manufacturers such as Dell, LG and Samsung, among others. Like Apple, Google has also created an application and content market but its cut is a more reasonable 10 per cent. Pearson was the first publisher to pull its content from iTunes in September 2011[25] in protest at paying such a significant chunk of revenues to Apple; other publishers are opting to develop advertising-only funded publications for iTunes to avoid having to share revenue with Apple.

Free market economists and advocates of the open web claim that any attempt to lock consumers into a proprietary infrastructure throttles growth. Consumer enthusiasm for Apple's iPad almost certainly kills that argument for now but publishers such as Pearson are voting with their feet. Technologists respond by arguing that it is only by a closed system and controlling access to content in a so-called 'walled garden' environment that publishers can generate reasonable margins. But a slew of new Android devices and a growing backlash from publishers unwilling to hand over a third of their revenues to Apple mean that Google could disrupt the market.

The future of media: smaller, leaner and less profitable

The debate about the future of traditional media has been taking place for the last decade. The business model for print with its huge supply chain is almost certainly flawed. Publishers are rushing to make their content available via digital channels. They are also looking to social media as a mechanism to enable readers to share content. What they have yet to figure out is

---

25 FT pulls app over customer data dispute with Apple, BBC News:
   http://www.bbc.co.uk/news/business-14734911

how to make money. Conventional media organisations will almost certainly be smaller and a lot leaner in future. There will be less money to be made. It's an issue that we'll continue to see played out over the next decade.

Summary

- The Internet has fundamentally changed the media business forever, removing the limitation on page count and deadline.
- But the Internet has also increased consumer appetite for content. Individuals access content via multiple formats, often consuming more than one media format at a time.
- Anyone with an Internet connection can become a publisher online and reach a global audience, providing that their content is sufficiently compelling.
- Social media has enabled the media industry to become truly participative but the lack of editorial rigour is a huge issue for corporate reputation.
- Traditional media owners are exploring numerous ways to generate revenue from digital content and there is a fight to own the distribution channel and relationship with the consumer.

CHAPTER

3

CHAPTER

CUTTING OUT THE MIDDLEMAN

The middleman of the media has changed. Now there are all sorts of media, everywhere. So what now? #brand anarchy

Some words just roll off the tongue. Like bubble, igloo, or yellow.

Disintermediation is not one of them. Economically speaking, it means the removal of intermediaries in a supply chain. In other words (and hence the title of this chapter), cutting out the middleman.

In most walks of life, this has meant deliberately bypassing the likes of distributors or agents in order to deal with the producer or supplier of goods or services directly. Good for the consumer, normally, and good for the supplier; but bad news for those in the middle, who suddenly find themselves short of business.

Apply this thinking to the new media landscape and you can see how social media enables brands to engage directly with audiences, thus cutting out the established middleman of conventional media, namely newspapers, magazines, radio and TV. Yet as far as reputation-forming is concerned, conventional media forms remain in a strong position in terms of creating influence. So is cutting out the media middleman – the 'barrier' of journalists and other conventional commentators that has existed for so long – a good or a bad thing for reputation, given that brands want to command the influence they have over their audiences? You might think it'd be a bad thing for reputation. But remember that brands have no control over conventional media and certainly don't have control over social forms of media – the aggravating factor here is the pace at which information, and therefore influence, now moves.

So control is not really the point: the point is making sense of the changed media landscape so you can formulate your approach. The challenge many brands are facing in doing that is that it has all changed so quickly, and so much fear, uncertainty and doubt are being raked up by industry watchers. Knowing how to approach the media turmoil is not easy. First though, there's the need to really get to grips with exactly what has been going on, and what this means for the future of media.

Maclaren: not all toddlers are equal – or are they?

On the morning of 8 November 2009, Farzad Rastegar, CEO of Maclaren, woke up to an email alerting him to a headline in the *New York Daily News* that read 'Maclaren stroller recall: firm recalls 1 million strollers on concerns children can cut off fingers'[1]. The pushchair manufacturer had planned to recall a million products following apparent finger injuries to 12 children caused by the hinges of two of its models. Maclaren had planned to make an announcement 24 hours later following guidance from the US Consumer Product Safety Commission (CPSC). But the story leaked.

Maclaren, by its own admission, was unprepared. According to Rastegar it had spent 'several months' developing a protective cover for the hinges. The story in the *Daily News* was inevitably picked up by other US media outlets and internationally via the web. It took the business several hours to issue a statement and because it had been caught out early it wasn't

---

1 Firm recalls 1 million strollers on concerns children can cut off fingers, New York Daily News, 8 November 2009: http://www.nydailynews.com/money/2009/11/09/2009-11-09_kid_stroller_can_cut_off_fingertips.html

equipped to deal with customers calling, emailing or visitors to its website seeking recall information.

Parents of young children are one of the most active demographics online. Inevitably the conversation moved to the blogosphere and Twitter as Maclaren customers 'called the company out'. Customers in the UK questioned whether they would be eligible for the recall. Maclaren's initial response was no. It said that its pushchairs conformed to European Union safety regulations and there had been only one reported injury in the UK. Concerned parents inevitably questioned the difference between the fingers of an American and a British toddler. Initially, Maclaren did not take any action to provide UK customers with the same hinge covers that were issued to US consumers, but following consumer pressure it relented.

Rastegar evaluated the crisis response effort of Maclaren in an article published in *Harvard Business Review*[2] in January 2011. He admitted, 'We were like athletes forced to play the big game a day early – in the rain. Everyone was out of breath. And things stayed that way for at least two weeks, until nearly all customer communications had been recovered and we were airlifting additional hinge covers from our production centre.'

The wall came down

Disintermediation, then. An ugly word, but one that spotlights the need for brands to distil various types of media down to some workable parts in order to best plan how to manage their reputations in future. The established media is no longer necessarily a brick wall between brands and their audiences. No more having to sweet-talk a journalist to convince them to

2 How I Did It: Maclaren's CEO on Learning from a Recall: http://hbr. org/2011/01/how-i-did-it-maclarens-ceo-on-learning-from-a-recall/ar/1

give you a quick mention in that story they're writing so that your reputation is enhanced.

Now you can go straight to the people, right into their living rooms, right onto their mobile phones, and right under their noses.

Bear in mind, though, that media has long given brands that kind of reach. People have long bought newspapers on the way to work or on the way home. They've watched TV while slumped on the sofa, they've listened to radio in their cars and, in more recent times, they've kept up with news and views on the Internet. Brands have long been in consumers' faces – it's just that the brands have not been able to 'watch'. And the audience has had, until now, few opportunities to answer back.

But here we are. A bruised but still highly influential conventional media that still, largely, has to work out how it will continue to make money; and a fast-growing, rowdy and ever-evolving social media that is hit and miss in the influence game. It can all blow over without blowing up, or it can tear into reputation with venom.

It is all too easy to see this as a shifting of the power base from established media barons and large publishing groups to networks of people with common interests who prefer to carry out their own analysis and form their own views. It is perhaps better to see it as a new opportunity – as the ability to have a different kind of media, and so a different kind of correspondence with brands, is now there. People are already seizing it with open arms, alongside the information that they gather from conventional media.

So, because of technology, the wall has come down. But the old world of media-in-the-middle remains extremely influential, although it is changing rapidly.

It's making sense of all this that is the big pig. Largely because the future of the conventional media is at stake in all of this while social media contributors are deliberately vociferous on this issue. Meaning that the range of views raised, exchanged, critiqued, tossed aside and fumbled with gingerly is immense: everyone wants to be in on the disintermediation debate. It's as if people haven't got enough to do with their time.

Does each media type need a different approach?

Meanwhile, brands sit back, draw breath and wonder how the routes to managing reputation through the creation of editorial influence have changed. Should conventional media remain a wall that must be climbed whereas social media needs smart, cautious engagement? Or is the matter more complicated than that? These two types of media have never been mutually exclusive, and given how they are beginning to cross over into each other's worlds, the whole picture continues to blur. In the future, and that won't be very far away, it will all just be media. Conventional and social. Direct and indirect. Middleman and man-to-man.

So, are the new instances of lack of middleman just all a muddle, man? Potentially, yes. Because this is all a hell of a lot more difficult than it used to be. Reputation management needs a new level of more sophisticated media planning, because each media – not just each type of media, each media – represents a different type of route to influence. And that impacts upon how brands engage editorially.

Here are a few examples.

Twitter

No middleman. Go directly to consumers, and remember that the appeal of your content is everything when it comes to sustaining brand engagement. Innovation is highly valued by the audience and can create knock-on appeal. Yet conventional journalists use Twitter too, so influence created on Twitter can have a bearing on the editorial they produce for conventional media consumption.

An established print magazine

The conventional editorial world remains a brick wall that brands must negotiate. The content is now also largely replicated online, but offers no openings for two-way reader engagement above and beyond that offered by the print magazine. Yet content is often highlighted and forwarded across social media networks. So influence is never just contained within the walls of the 'publication' – because the content is on the Internet too, it can be spread across all forms of media, albeit that paywalls and subscriber access requirements will inhibit its impact.

A progressive national newspaper

It has a foot in both camps: it publishes in print, but publishes even more content online. It doesn't yet charge for any of the online content, but in the future it will. It uses Facebook to cement its audience following, and understands the power that its branded content can have when it finds its way into social media. It has its own branded media, in the shape of a YouTube channel. Many of its journalists use Twitter personally and professionally. So the conventional media elements remain an indirect, or associated, way of creating influence – the editorial factor is required to make the influence more forceful if brands are to develop better reputation. The newspaper's brand certainly counts for something influence-wise. Yet it is very fragmented: there are often several social media avenues under the same roof – for example feeds used by individual journalists, as branded feeds from separate sections of the publication and for the overall newspaper. And given that the same people are delivering content across all of those mediums, the lines are blurred so far as to be practically invisible anyway. So influence through editorial is controlled by journalists across both conventional and social media platforms; plus consumers can engage directly both with the media brands and with other brands that are featured in the content that appears, for example in the comment stream below an article about a certain brand. There's a need for intricate planning, but herein lie the willing ingredients of a highly potent influence mix.

And there is another factor, and probably a far more important one. Editorial control and the barriers to creating influence are complicated; they require a new level of planning. But that just gets you in the door: once you're in and ready to engage, there's a whole series of conversations to have. Make or break conversations.

This new level of planning is pretty foreign to most marketers let alone most PRs; and it's incredibly complicated in comparison to how we did things in years gone by. But it's crucial. The question is where to start.

It's best, like with any media campaign, to take the broadest possible look at the mix of relevant and available media to work with. But rather than looking at all the different forms of media that now exist and trying to categorise them in niches for the sake of familiarity – like individual social media platforms, local weekly newspapers or corporate websites — the people responsible for planning and managing influence through editorial are better off looking at how different forms of media 'function' in the minds of audiences. This approach is becoming more commonplace as the development of influence, albeit at lightning pace, across different, digitised media becomes better understood, and communicators begin to learn from brands that have set precedents. Rather than a multitude of media niches, start with earned, bought and branded media.

Each of these forms of media has brand reputation value in its own right. What a brand communicates about itself directly, via its 'own' media, will influence reputation – particularly if it's a ham-fisted attempt to gain influence that is counterproductive, or a brilliantly executed piece of content that demonstrates empathy with the audience. 'Bought' media – or content published and controlled by the brand itself – can influence reputation far above and beyond the immediate commercial intentions of its content. Think back to television commercials from your youth that still live large in the memory today, and then think about how they influence(d) your perception of those brands.

Looking instead at earned media, its potential to influence the audience lies right at the heart of public relations – there is inherent value in recommendation or reference having more power. This is because it's not the organisation saying it, it's a third party. It's perceived as not having a direct commercial agenda – through that perception can, of course, be misplaced.

So branded media, or 'owned' media as it is sometimes called, has the advantage of the content being under the editorial control of the brand itself. Yet the dialogue with the audience about that content, the stuff that can be really influential, can be in the hands of another party if it's a social media platform – for example, a branded YouTube channel. The editorial control of branded media is also its disadvantage, in that it can lack credibility unless it's done right.

But the fact that it's effectively the brand's mouthpiece is a card that can be played to its advantage, depending on the subject matter and the level of audience scrutiny. Owned media has enormous potential power to develop and maintain brand awareness, and it can foster trust and belief too, through creative techniques borne of knowing as much as possible about what might compel the audience to buy. It can create or change impressions of brands in the minds of the audience. Earned media – the stuff generated through the conventional press – has the ability to create similar outcomes and also has the advantage of potentially greater influence because of the editorial factor and the reach of the information. But planning and achieving those editorial outcomes is a constant challenge, as potency and suitability of content are the route to success.

Finding common ground

There is one common thread, from a planning perspective, that connects all three media disciplines: understanding the audience. It might sound like the most obvious statement, but if you know the audience inside out you can best figure out what will be most effective.

To know how best to communicate to the advantage of the brand, you've got to know what to say and how to say it. That's always been true in the business of public relations, it's just now a much, much bigger job. But we are armed with more prescriptive tools with which to do it.

Nestlé loses Face(book)

Nestlé was caught in the eye of a very public storm when its Facebook fan page became overrun with comments from environmental protestors and sustainability watchers. Despite its efforts to engage with the public directly and build engagement for its master brand, the firm instead found itself publicly exposed to direct criticism, and unable to handle that conversation effectively. The conversation was rooted in criticism, and appeared to have been a coordinated effort.

It started with Greenpeace posting a spoof video online that criticised the Kit-Kat brand and Nestlé's claimed use of palm oil.

Then it moved to Facebook. The initial response from Nestlé was to remove comments from its Facebook page that criticised its business. So the conversation went silent. But then to make matters worse, Nestlé posted its own comments seeking to justify why it had done the editing job, openly criticising its detractors with what by anyone's standards is a pretty harsh tone.

It turned an increasingly sour chat into a public row[3]. There has been much analysis of how Nestlé handled the conversation and what it could have done better to tackle the comments head-on rather than seeking to remove them[4]. One major highlight – or lowlight – was the company's apparent use of someone in a junior position to write and manage its comments.

By responding more appropriately rather than being provoked, by not seeking to sanction comment but discussing it openly, and by not rising to Greenpeace's bait, Nestlé could have gained reputation points rather than seen its actions held up as an example of how not to engage audiences.

Conversation: an art

In theory at least, brands should be entirely comfortable with conversation. For decades they have been seeking closer connections with their audiences, a lingering emotive umbilical cord between the consumer and the producer, a genuine and lasting relationship in which there's mutual respect, a camaraderie

---

3 Nestlé mess shows sticky side of Facebook pages, CNET: http://news.cnet. com/8301-13577_3-20000805-36.html
4 How to salvage your brand on Facebook: lessons for Nestle, Social Media Today: http://socialmediatoday.com/index.php?q=SMC/183947

and an unflinching desire to ensure that what it produces is exactly what the consumer wishes to consume, profitably.

In reality, the Internet's ability to enable consumers and brands to interact directly has caught brands on the hop. Rather than being suave and sympathetic conversationalists, most brands have found themselves either occasional participants in debates or information circulars that they have little influence over, unless they started them in the first place. Like reputation management writ-large, conversation is very much an art rather than a science.

So it's all about the art of conversation? Well, surely an outgoing brand stuffed full of marketing talent, with global recognition and respect, would have no problem holding conversations? After all, it holds conversations about itself, its products, its markets and its audiences every minute of every day. They're internal, they're through conventional marketing channels like advertising and media relations, they're with customers and partners, and they're with shareholders. They're with anyone who'll listen. Surely conversations started, developed and sustained using social media can just be a bolt-on extension of all that information exchange that is already swilling around all over the place?

Surely this is all relatively easy? The art of conversation is something best undertaken and exploited by the most accomplished and engaging conversationalists in the organisation – the most senior people; those with direct responsibility for the important operations, those who already interact with customers in order to do their jobs. It's all great news: we can now talk to all our audiences in a way that they'll listen to. We can, in a virtual sense, walk right up to them, tell them things that will influence them and do things that will impress them. Like the ultimate chat-up situation in a bar full of compliant and willing suitors.

It's a wonderful theory, but if it were true then most brands wouldn't be struggling to assess and contain the bleating and tweeting of all of their employees on social media, or work out how on earth they try to hold productive and meaningful conversations online as an organisation rather than cowering in the face of attacks from the disgruntled. The art of conversation needs a very different application in social media-land than in person or, one step removed, via conventional media. Because the rules have not only changed, they have morphed into an entirely new set of rules, for a type of media that brands have never had to work with before. It is not just a major shift like the dawn of television broadcasting, it is a wholly different thing altogether. It is less of a tool and more of a weapon.

The daunting scale of conversations

Social media has not only created new opportunities to engage with audiences but has also made the whole area of reputation management more complicated, not least because there is so much more to manage now. Equally though, the direct and conversational nature of, in particular, Twitter means that brands can have a far more accurate and immediate barometer of customer opinion about themselves and their activities. It means that reputations can be built at lightning pace, but it also means that they can crumble even faster. At least brands have the scope to influence their own reputations directly though, providing they know what they're doing and can live at the pace of the conversation. Like the well-worn analogy, social media engagement can be much like conversations in a bar or pub: flitting between serious and frivolous, noisy and quiet, one-to-one or small groups or large groups, and with the tendency to alter direction in the blink of an eye.

Which is why any brand expert worth their salt has been quick to point out that engaging with customers using social media is all about listening. It is a good point, and probably the most rudimentary one that organisations have to grasp. They must not only listen to what is going on around them and about them, but also listen to customers and groups of customers when they do step forward and 'talk' to the brand. Yet it is not all about listening – the ability to listen and act upon conversations is just one side of the coin. The other, in keeping with those pub and park scenarios of the real world, is to open your mouth and say something. It will make sure you have a voice that can be listened to but, like a first-timer in the local boozer, many brands can be unsure of what to say or what the consequences of piping up may be. Instead, they remain on the fringes of the conversation, smiling sweetly and nodding at others, but not scoring any points themselves — they are more observers than participants.

The art of social media conversation is an art, not a science. But it does require some basic science to be effective – brands need a mouth as well as ears, and an acute sense of smell can come in handy too. Particularly when conversations are likely to snowball, and extend beyond social media into physical conversations and somewhere where the snowball can become an avalanche, the good old conventional media.

The mighty media mashup

You can cut out the middleman if you deal with social media. But your conversations are visible to anyone with a connection to the Internet, so you can't stop conventional media picking up on what you have published and then publishing reports on your content. Not just a straightforward report of the proceedings either: it's more likely to be the press interpretation of what's happening online, which is then in turn analysed, sensationalised and contextualised according to media agenda and, depending on the scenario, raked up every time journalists want to illustrate or reinforce a point.

A few years ago, journalists were not really that bothered about social media. It was an interesting development, it could help them monitor and research stories, they may have even had a personal passion for something and – being the sort of people who like writing things and expressing opinions – either written or contributed to some blogs. Since then, as Facebook in particular has expanded its appeal around the world, the conventional media has realised that social media is no longer a special interest. It is mainstream and, while not everyone is online and not everyone publishes content, it is a reasonable reflection of public opinion and interest. The light bulb moment in Fleet Street[5] happened a while ago.

The title of this section contains the word 'mashup'[6]. Let's be clear, 'mashup' is not actually a real word, regardless of any attempts to gain it a place in the dictionary. In social media terms, it seems to mean everything from pulling two data streams together (think of those scenes with the proton packs at the end of *Ghostbusters*[7]) to a few nerds using the word 'cool' a lot over a chai latte.

We've used the godforsaken word here in a tongue-in-cheek way, to illustrate that conventional and social media are beginning to blend together, and will ultimately merge permanently, creating a media that often connects brands directly with consumers, but which can also be indirect, and which leaves an audit trail and so changes the rules of engagement. We are not there yet: some newspapers use their websites to do little more than replicate online the content that they publish offline. But the more progressive media companies

---

5   The Fleet Street revolution (Media UK): www.mediauk.com/article/32718/
    the-fleet-street-revolution
6   Mashup (Wordnik): www.wordnik.com/words/mashup
7   Ghostbusters movie: http://ghostbusters.com/

are setting the pace, both with online content that engages readers in a richer experience and pulls multiple types of social media content into the frame, and offline content – think glossy magazines – that is published shrewdly in order to maximise its potency for social media.

So the media mashup is just beginning, and although the moguls are now getting serious about needing to make readers pay for content, the change in commercial models is embryonic. Over time, social media platforms may shine and fade, but the ability to connect directly means it is here to stay, in some form. Which in turn means that conventional media will simply have to evolve to meet changing reader expectations. The picture remains cloudy, but you'd have to be pretty short-sighted to believe that social media will take over the world and that today's media barons will just retire early. Instead, it will all just be media: a new, more engaging and more powerful form of it.

What do these media trends mean for brands, though, now and in the future? Well it's certainly a series of developments that need to be watched closely, which few brands did well in the early days of social media. We are seeing the biggest change in the media since the invention of the printing press, and that has manifold implications for every brand. Yet we won't have the full picture until conventional and social media are joined firmly at the hip.

In the meantime, the most important thing is for brands to take a joined-up approach to how they handle their reputations across conventional and social media, rather than getting dazzled by digitisation or, instead, sticking solely to the familiarity of regular media.

The risks of concentrating on one camp alone are pretty stark. Rather than developing an understanding of how the two genres interlace, and how content can gain visibility and evolve when it is unleashed across the two, brands can be blindsided by, for example, the way in which a social media campaign is analysed and documented by a national newspaper or, conversely, how an attempt to plug a brand in newspapers through a well-worn publicity tactic starts attracting a groundswell of criticism across social media.

In particular, abandoning conventional media and taking the direct route to consumers means that brands forego any influence they may have had over journalists. That is the kind of approach that does not deliver control; instead it thoroughly undermines it.

Media everywhere: mobile, static, work and play

It is not just the shape of the media that needs to be considered though. It's also the delivery of media content. And unless you've been living in a cave for the past few years, a cave without a high-speed broadband connection, 3G network access and an IP address that is, you'll have noticed that there are many more devices on which people can read stories and view videos these days. And much is going on to ensure that both conventional and social media content can be delivered anytime, anywhere, on anything.

There is an army of media experts and geeks out there who debate the pros and cons of digesting content on each new platform that emerges. There are obvious points like whether the stuff is too small to see. But there are the deeper issues such as download speed, the practicality of viewing content while on the move, scope for reader engagement, scope for that engagement to be seamless across different devices, operating system compatibility shenanigans, and the hoary old chestnut of navigability.

Which is all interesting stuff worthy of debate as technological change continues to drive media change. But the broader point is perhaps of greater value to brands, both in getting to grips with reputation now and planning for the future. It is that media, all media, is everywhere. All the time. On display in public places, in people's homes, at their workplaces, in the palms of their hands. You cannot escape it, and the sheer availability and potency of information is such that most readers don't want to escape it. They practically have a bloodlust for news and conversation.

For brands, there are two overarching factors to consider in working out the reputational implications: *where* people consume media, and *how* they do it.

Let's look at the 'where' part first. Media used to be in your hands, in the form of a newspaper or other journal. Then it expanded to the airwaves with the arrival of public wireless broadcasting, and then swiftly on to the television screen. The Internet obviously began to change all that. Initially though, the exciting development was just immediacy: text-based news reports could be read on websites at any time, so web-based media could break stories faster than the television or radio news channels. In effect, the Internet killed the newsflash.

Yet for much of the 1990s, media consumption over the Internet largely took place at a PC in the home or in the office. In the second half of the decade, more and more office workers got laptops rather than bulky desktops, but wi-fi was not yet available and the prospect of dialling up over a phone line to slowly download a news report didn't fill most of us with joy. There were early news alert services and ticker applications that were useful in news monitoring, but which hardly represented a pleasant and engaging way to consume media content.

It was, by and large, the arrival of faster wireless networks that changed all that. It meant that phones could download data faster and so provide us with richer content while on the move.

It meant – in urban and suburban areas at least – the widespread availability of reasonably quick fixed-line broadband and wi-fi services so that using a laptop to get media information became practical as opposed to a kerfuffle. The hype has always looked to the future and anyone who was subjected to the promise and frustration of WAP on 2G mobile phone a decade ago will attest that readers were initially let down by the technology. Now though, with the ubiquity of 3G phones, the looming arrival of 4G, and a social shift that has seen people using laptops, and now iPads, in all manner of places, the promise has become a reality. And because of social media, readers aren't just viewing the content; they're commenting on it and creating it. In many cases, they are part of the headlines, rather than being subjected to them following a nervy two-minute dial-up download.

People used to get the news by reading a paper over breakfast or on the way to work, or by listening to the radio while behind the wheel or watching TV in the evenings. Apart from the dawn of breakfast TV and, more importantly, 24-hour media coverage thanks to the arrival of satellite networks, not too much changed between that paper over breakfast and the arrival of the first Internet news sites. But today, people are reading about, sharing information about and engaging with brands on trains, in pubs, at their desks, on the beach, in the queue for the cashpoint and in the loo. Yes, in the loo.

Media consumption takes place while readers are static *and* mobile. It used to make a big difference, as the captive audience traits of the evening TV news, for example, made it enormously influential, while people in transit were often only exposed to brands in relatively fleeting glimpses – apart from British rail passengers of course, who could find themselves stuck on platforms with far more time to read the papers than they'd intended. Today, it is practically irrelevant whether the reader is sat still or on the move. Media consumption is pretty much constant throughout each day for some people, apart from when they're asleep. In the future, even more people will consume media this way, albeit with attention spans and the capacity to be influenced varying depending on what they're looking at, where they are and how much of what they hear and see matters to them. Location is no longer a factor in determining what impact a media message will create; instead, for brand reputation managers, harnessing audience attention and engagement are much more important.

Then there is the issue of how people consume media. Again though, the distinctions between different platforms are breaking down as publishers tailor content to the devices their readers are using and software developers innovate so that media can be consumed in a practical way on many types of devices.

Just as location has become irrelevant, so devices used to consume content are becoming less important to brand reputation managers. Of course, it matters very much to the consumer: whether they're listening to the radio, tweeting on a 3G phone or relaxing with a Sunday travel supplement before the kids come back from the park, the media platform has a bearing on the reader's experience and so its impact on influence – and thus reputation – may vary. This is something that brands are starting to get to grips with, as more precise content planning is undertaken so that there is a better understanding of the desired editorial outcomes.

The bigger picture, though, is that while consumer experiences vary by platform, content can infiltrate any platform – and most consumers are accessing it via several platforms. Any thoughts of a consumer getting a raw deal because they're struggling to view expansive video content on a phone screen should be banished – if they care, then before the day is out they'll have found another way to view it.

Have appetites changed?

What brands are having to understand, and what social media gives them better insight into, is that human beings consume media content throughout each day, both when they have a quiet moment to focus on it and when they're wrapped up in doing several things at once.

Just as media planners had to get to grips with the various types of conventional media that could influence consumers during the average day – perhaps waking up to radio, a bit of TV news during breakfast, a newspaper or news summary on the BlackBerry® on the train, then Internet news grazing during the working day and the lot in reverse in the evening – so those horizons now need to expand to social media as well. Moreover, the way in which content is received, commented on, forwarded and so evolves across different types of media needs close scrutiny.

The challenge for brands now is not really that different to the challenges they've had to face in the past couple of decades – much more media, many more options, far more ground to cover. It is just that the scale of the job has increased beyond prior comprehension because of social media. And there's the added challenge of it offering dialogue rather than monologue. Engagement with brands is no longer a series of quick hits; it must be sustained.

Recall the Toyota thing?

Toyota, a vehicle brand with a once enviable reputation for product quality, has found out in no uncertain terms that relying on conventional media alone in the wake of a crisis can be problematic.

The company has experienced several years of major product recall incidents, each one played out before not just a watching media, but a growing audience base connected to the brand – and to each other – directly by social media. In the largest of the incidents, the firm recalled four million cars in the autumn of 2009 amidst fears of sticking problems with accelerator pedals. Four months later, it extended the recall to a further 2.3 million cards over similar technical concerns. Then in 2010, a combined 2.6 million further cars, of different models, were recalled over an engine control system, brake and fuel pump defects. Around six months later, fuel leakage worries saw another 1.7 million recalled.

It is stating the obvious, but that's a lot of cars, even for the world's largest carmaker.

The furore is often held up as an example[8] of a brand that had direct engagement with its audience already using social media, but ignored that in how it responded to the crisis, and suffered a resulting backlash.

While, if you look at the statistics, Toyota appears to have been highly, directly engaged with its audiences using social media during the recall period and afterwards, it has been roundly criticised for not delivering the content – and the transparency – that could have otherwise restricted the damage to its reputation[9]. The content was there, but commentators[10] have pointed out that it was not there early enough, and engaging people in frank conversations about

---

8 Toyota's reputation could be tarnished for years, BBC News: http://news. bbc.co.uk/1/hi/business/8498036.stm

9 Is Toyota's reputation finished?, Business Week; http://www.businessweek. com/lifestyle/content/jan2010/bw20100128_413922.htm

10 Toyota's recall and crisis management 2.0 http://sparxoo.com/2010/01/29/ toyotas-recall-and-crisis-management-2-0/

the situation and intended remedy earlier rather than facing criticism over apparent opacity would have helped to keep the situation from boiling over. As the recall situation unfolded, information was released progressively through the company's website and conventional media relations. But by not mobilising the consumers who were connected to Toyota online already, many of whom therefore had the potential to be positive brand ambassadors, it's easy to think that the company was digging in the wrong places in its bid to communicate its way through the crisis.

It then went on to try to engage those people again post-crisis, using a micro-site about the product recalls so it could put its side of the story clearly and simply. By then though, many observers saw it as too little, too late.

They're listening. What now?

Today's fragmented media is a very different environment in which to manage reputation compared to the past. Previously, brands would orchestrate communication that largely amounted to preparing blocks of predominantly self-serving content which was then released, shrewdly, to media contacts and supported by regulated access to spokespeople for interviews. Not that brands really had much choice – those were the media options available, so it was a case of working those outlets to the best of their ability, keeping what they didn't want to make public well under wraps and maintaining what was, in comparison with the two-way Internet age, a narrow field of communication with the outside world.

This means that influence upon reputation, because of the editorial control maintained by conventional media, was something of a game of chance. There have been many well-plotted exercises to release information that created maximum attention for a brand, and stirs word-of-mouth by sensationalising the subject or the information. They tended to take the tried-and-tested approach of assessing the media's editorial appetites and doing such a comprehensive job of preparing content that journalists essentially took the whole package – it was simply too good a story to turn down or even meddle with very much – and 'control' over those particular elements of reputation building was highly effective. They could second-guess how stories would develop in the media, what deadlines they'd work to, how coverage was likely to spread across daily newspapers, daytime and evening TV and radio bulletins, and be assessed through more analytical editorial columns over time.

The Internet has, fairly obviously, upped the pace beyond anything conceivable just 20 years ago. Now the stories develop far faster. But the main shift in how brands need to respond to these changes is that media is now a two-way street, and the audience can play an active role in the story that is communicated externally. It is perhaps surprising, given the rapid rise of the Internet as part of the fabric of our lives, to think back to how the media was before it.

Then, apart from letters to the editor, the way in which the public participated in editorial was really just restricted to the broadcast vox pop, or the journalist interviewing the eye-witness in the street about an event or their opinions on something important. Yet even that was highly controlled, subject to both editorial standards and whims, and gave an ultra-slim view of what the audience really thought or knew. And it could be subject to distortion.

Today, the public can actively change the course of reporting in the conventional media, and alter perception and reputation because of content and comments shared across social media.

While in the early days of social media this was touted as 'citizen journalism', it now seems generally accepted that this is just one element of the way in which the audience can be engaged in the editorial process. The audience has, en masse, an element of editorial control over perception and so, ultimately, over reputation. Which, given that they ultimately determine what your reputation is, could either be a good thing or a bad thing.

For the corporation or governmental organisation, this means that it's no longer really acceptable, let alone effective, to issue a well-worded communiqué, then sit back and wait for publicity, or a reaction. This factor is at the heart of how the reputation game has changed.

Engagement means the prospect of a direct connection between brand and consumer, a connection that is all too easy to orchestrate. But those connections are also forged with rivals, protestors, politicians, shareholders; in fact anyone with an Internet connection. So it's about more than simply being connected: it's about expectation, transparency, clarity and most important of all – behaviour. Not just how a brand behaves in the eyes of the watching public and media in a specific instance, but its cumulative behaviour over the long haul. And in managing its behaviour, a brand is far more exposed to risk that it has ever been.

BlackBerry bruised

Despite the popularity of the iPhone and the rise of Android devices, Research in Motion's (RIM) BlackBerry remains a dominant mobile email platform for business with more than 70 million users[11]. But its reputation was badly bruised when

---

11 BlackBerry outage for three days caused by faulty router says former RIM staffer, The Guardian, 14 October 2011: http://www.guardian.co.uk/technology/2011/Oct/14/BlackBerry-outage-faulty-router-suspected

its email service failed for four days in October 2011. The failure meant that emails, messages and web browsing were all intermittent. If your company's service is the provision of secure information access on the move, a serious outage will inevitably hit customer confidence. The failure apparently resulted from the upgrade to a server at the company's European headquarters in Slough, UK.

In responding to the crisis, it appeared that RIM's communication effort was being directed by its legal team rather than the communication team. RIM did little to explain the issue beyond issuing brief statements acknowledging the failure until day three of the crisis, when the issue began to have an impact on customers worldwide. Among those customers were many of the world's media who used their outlets to describe RIM's efforts to deal with the situation. RIM's CEO for UK and Ireland, Stephen Bates, said that engineers were working around the clock to get to the bottom of the problem.

Customers, many of them high profile, turned to Twitter to vent their fury at RIM's lack of communication about what was being done to fix the issue and how long it was likely to take. The failure was repeatedly a trending topic over the four days of the crisis and disaffected customers used the hashtag #dearblackberry to tag their tweets. The long-term damage to the business will be revealed in the months to come. Inevitably businesses that chose RIM because of its reliability are looking at other communication platforms.

But in principle, engagement in the editorial world, and directly with the audience, is an extremely positive development. So they're listening, and you're listening, and you're both communicating. A new kind of editorial control is being applied to these conversations to ensure that you're both addressing concerns and negative situations, and nurturing positive perception. You're engaged in a new level of reputation management, one that is more sophisticated, more demanding and potentially more fruitful, but more perilous, than the world of conventional media alone. You're actively conversing. Do it right and you can gain greater command of your brand reputation. The question is, what lies beyond this as media continues to digitise and communicators continue to innovate?

A world of influence beyond engagement

The answer lies in the depth of engagement. There is potential to go beyond managing and milking the implications of editorial for your brand by being closely engaged to consumers and the media. There is the prospect of being able to participate with them. The fairly functional management of new kinds of two-way communication, required because the audience is now engaged, is a big step forward for a brand and it can be very successful. But to take greater command of conversations in a way that recognises and is sympathetic to the role of the audience in determining the 'story' of the brand goes further, and can be more powerful in shaping reputation. This puts content right under the microscope – the extent to which it is going to be trusted and the degree to which it can cement belief must be fully understood.

This kind of participation in reputation will require a whole new level of sophistication. It will require organisations to have communication as their operational oxygen. It will require a 360-degree understanding of the audience, bravery underpinned by systemic command, and control systems to authorise instantaneous content. It needs a plan.

According to the Francis Ingham, director general of the Public Relation Consultants Association (PRCA), communicators are being forced to up their game with more effective planning. Not just because media now demands it, but because they've never been much good at it.

'The public relations industry is typically pretty lousy at the planning process. Being able to segment, and so target, an audience well is something public relations needs to get better at but the more important need is to get better at planning overall. If we're going to make public relations more valuable then we need to get even better at it than the advertising world. Planning is one of the best investments that public relations agencies can make at the moment,' he says. 'But segmentation needs to be approached sensibly. We can delude ourselves into thinking that we are more sophisticated at this than we are. Segmentation by conventional means will only get you so far when you're dealing with editorial. We need more pragmatism and less hot air when it comes to segmenting audiences, particularly when using social media,' he adds.

Integrated media planning

If you've been sat there thinking 'what is needed is some really grown-up, intricate and pragmatic planning', you're not wrong.

But what is not needed is another layer – social media planning in addition to conventional media planning misses the point, and adds a layer of unnecessary complexity without the required consideration to the relationship between the two. And as this book has been preaching for the past few chapters, before long it will all just be media. A bigger, more engaging, two-way and one-way, available everywhere and lightning-speed media; but media nonetheless. The distinction between social and conventional platforms will fall away.

For the meantime though, each type of media will need a distinct approach, as part of a single, overarching reputation content plan. The format and scope will vary by brand, but the basic parameters are a long-term view of how reputation can best be built, what factors will accelerate that reputational development, who the audiences are and what content is required to exert appropriate command over influence. In some ways, there is much that public relations can learn from advertising here: the ad world has long had a professional, detail-driven approach to planning and rightly so, given that clients are paying for the media space they occupy. In public relations, the need has never been so acute, given that editorial content influenced by organisations has no ultimate assurances over where and when it is used. A comprehensive plan detailing intended space, story angle, treatment and, ideally, headline adds much sophistication to the typical public relations campaign, but can only get you so far.

Reputation content plans are a new frontier for public relations planning, a discipline that, in all too many cases, has either failed to grasp the interrelationship between editorial and other types of content or, at the worst end of the spectrum, applies techniques that can't really qualify as planning at all. These plans must take a microscope to the probable short-term outcomes of customer and media engagement through editorial, but must do so in the context of brand reputation and brand relationships in the longer term. Success therein is dependent on the expertise of people who really know what they're doing with reputation. It needs a thorough understanding of appetite for and timing of editorial, its likely implications once 'public' and the associated implications for the brand. Which is where public relations nous has its biggest role to play in customer engagement – editorial savvy is needed in spades.

Overall, though, no plan can be too rigid given the media upheaval that is under way, and the requirement for sheer agility that has been created by direct dialogue with audiences. But you've got to start somewhere. And you've got to start by gaining a 360-degree view of what media could conceivably influence your reputation, then narrow your vision to those best suited and with the greatest potency, and *then* start plotting content. In tandem with that, there is a need for a far more agile approach within the organisation to enhancing reputation through editorial influence.

Finally, there is a need for a different mindset to be applied to this different media landscape. Brand leaders may be worried about social media because they fear loss of control, but they never really had control. With conventional media, they could at least plan content and nurture relationships so that they commanded attention, even if they didn't control the editorial output. By doing so, they could set or participate in the media agenda. Now the media agenda is in so many more hands, and opinions can change like the wind.

Whether there's a media middleman or not, only the level of content planning and operational agility that come with editorial understanding can turn a potentially perilous fumble in the dark into the ability to exercise some command over reputation. It is a big step up from dealing purely with conventional media and the approach is a departure from what marketing departments have historically been used to. Chief amongst the factors they have to come to terms with is that every consumer potentially has the brand in its sights, and can publish a reaction to it.

Planning and media savvy put to one side, we come to the issues of credibility and, ultimately, truth. Reputation is worth nothing if there is no trust. And recent media changes do not sit comfortably with the conventional spin doctor. Indeed, the spin doctor's blend of medicine might be the last thing that brands need.

Summary

- The previous barrier between brands and their audiences that was created by the media as we knew it has now eroded.
- This makes two-way conversation with audiences possible, but the challenge can be knowing what to say and where to begin.
- Media has become a complex landscape and content, and therefore influence can flow quickly across the different types.
- Not only that, but media can be instantaneous and available everywhere, so agility is paramount in reputation management efforts.
- Once you have audiences engaged in conversation with you, what do you do next?.
- Why more mature, more expansive planning is required so that content and conversations can have a more strategic bearing on reputation.

CHAPTER

4

THE END OF SPIN AND THE NEED FOR AUTHENTIC COMMUNICATION

The Internet has killed spin forever. Transparency is the only possibly form of sustainable organisational communication. #brandanarchy

'The best way to build a reputation is to deserve it.'
Seth Godin

Media fragmentation and the rise of Internet-driven communication is returning public relations to its roots as a means for an organisation to engage with the public in a two-way process. Yet the public relations industry is locked into systems and processes that have become industrialised over the past 50 years. But change is coming, and fast. You have been warned.

It is no longer possible to control or dominate a media agenda. Arguably it never has been, although you're about to read about one communications practitioner that retained an iron grip on the media for half a decade. The simple fact is that the public relations and communications practitioners are no longer in control, or in what they thought was control. You'll almost certainly be bored of hearing that mantra by the time you have read this book. It's message that runs through it like words through a stick of Blackpool rock.

Alastair Campbell[1] is best known for his role as former British Prime Minister Tony Blair's spokesman, press secretary and

---

1 Alastair Campbell's personal website: www.alastaircampbell.org/

director of communications and strategy from 1997 to 2003, having started working for Blair in 1994. According to Campbell, it is no longer possible to control a media agenda. The style of communication planning that characterised his tenure in Downing Street no longer works. But with a handful of newspapers, fewer broadcast outlets and limited online publications, it used to be far easier to set and lead a media agenda. In the mid-1990s, a hit on BBC News coupled with a splash in *The Sun* and *The Times* would ensure that a story dominated the agenda for at least 24 hours. Blair's first election win in 1997, and subsequent re-election landslide in 2001, were built on this command and control approach to communications. We met Campbell when he spoke to a group of communications professionals at a dinner in London, organised by media evaluation firm Durrants, while we were researching this book.

Snagging the attention of the BBC and national newspapers helps, of course, but there are dozens of other influential channels that have equal clout and are vying for the same audience. 'It used to be fairly straightforward working out how to dominate the agenda – get yourself on the main news, and big in a few of the papers, and everything else would flow. But companies and individuals in the public eye have had to adapt to a totally changed media landscape in which the old rules no longer apply in the same way. The way media is digitising, and the pace at which it has already happened, has changed the game for those wanting to be out there connecting with the public. It now means understanding all media channels, knowing which will be most potent, and how they can work in unison. And it means letting go of the belief that "the agenda" can be controlled. The agenda is being set as much by those who consume the media – and respond instantly – as those who are trying to exert that control,' says Campbell. He continues: 'This means public relations techniques have to adapt constantly. Digital media and, in particular, social media have injected new requirements for transparency, detailed story planning and genuine dialogue with the audience. Now, the audiences can get involved in the editorial coverage of the issue – they can talk back, and sometimes their responses can be more interesting and more newsworthy than the initial point. Information must be both authentic and delivered with full appreciation of how the audience is most likely to react.'

Campbell says that we have entered the era of the permanent campaigning, citing five organisational communication themes that demand a fundament shift in communication style to what he called 'authentic campaigning'[2].

Alastair Campbell's five organisational communication themes

Citizens and consumers

Private sector standards and efficiencies are expected of the public sector, and public sector values are expected of the private sector. This shift has made it much harder to operate in both the private and public sectors.

Rise of the democratic corporation

Stakeholders are no longer clearly defined. The Internet provides a window through which organisations can be scrutinised minute-by-minute. This has completely changed corporate democracy.

---

2 Command and control communication planning gives way to authentic campaigning, says Alastair Campbell, Speed Communications blog post: www.speedcommunications.com/blogs/wadds/2009/09/20/ command-and-control-communication-planning-gives-way-to-authentic-campaigning-says-alastair-campbell

Participatory media environment

Print can't deal with a 24-hour news culture and its web-based response is leading to financial ruin. Newspapers are still important and still set the agenda for broadcasters, but social media is cutting through, particularly with big stories.

Culture of negativity

Negativity drives the media. In 1974, for every one negative story there were three positive; by 2003, Campbell claimed the ratio had switched to 18 negative for every one positive. It's a tough environment in which to operate.

Information is infinity

A strong, clear message pushed to one or two sources is no longer good enough for successful communications. We operate in an era of infinite sources and infinite channels.

New organisational influence flows

The major shift in the last decade that underpins almost all of Campbell's themes is technology. The Internet provides the means for an organisation to engage directly with the public. This new media is social and, as Campbell acknowledges, it is participatory. This is the basic premise that provides the basis for Philip Sheldrake's book *The Business of Influence*[3]. Sheldrake is an engineer turned public relations practitioner who brings a refreshing perspective to organisational communication. 'Information and communication technology has laid bare the facts in a way that you can't call anything less than brutal these days. You can't fake it so, to me, reality is now perception. So

---

3 *The Business of Influence* (Philip Sheldrake): www.influenceprofessional. com Wiley, 2011.

you'd better make sure you build that reality in order to live up to the perception you'd like others to have of you. Ultimately that's the business of influence,' he says.

In *The Business of Influence*, Sheldrake challenges his readers to reconsider the influence flows around an organisation. In his reframing of organisation communication he identifies six primary influence flows:

1. Our influence with our stakeholders
2. Our stakeholders' influence with each other with respect to us
3. Our stakeholders' influence with us
4. Our competition's influence with stakeholders
5. Stakeholders' influence with each other with respect to our competitors
6. Stakeholders' influence with our competition

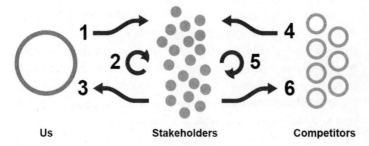

Us   **Stakeholders**   **Competitors**

Figure: Philip Sheldrake's Six Influence Flows

Sheldrake's contention is that the first flow (our influence with our stakeholders) and the corresponding third flow (our stakeholders' influence with us) are well understood and these are the typically the areas where an organisation will invest the majority of its marketing and sales effort. But technology has made the second flow critical to the management of the reputation of an organisation and your market online. Your stakeholders are using the Internet to find each other and communicate about your organisation online. You need to find those conversations as they will almost certainly provide incredible insight about your organisation and you may decide that your organisation needs to be part of those conversations. Equally, technology makes it easier to track your competitors and their influence on your stakeholders and vice versa – influence flows 4, 5 and 6. Organisations must also track these conversations and be aware of their reputational impact.

Radical transparency

What will you do when your organisation's file servers are turned over to the Internet and your most confidential documents are available for anyone to view and copy? If you don't think it will happen, think again. It has happened to the US government on more than one occasion. Wikileaks[4] is a non-profit media organisation that publishes private and classified information from anonymous news sources, news leaks and whistle-blowers. In April 2010, it published footage from a 2007 Baghdad airstrike in which a dozen people, including two journalists, were allegedly killed by gunfire from a helicopter[5]. Throughout 2010, it released US government information from the wars in Afghanistan and Iraq and then in November 2010 it began leaking US diplomatic cables[6]. Wikileaks is the harsh reality of the future of Internet transparency that organisations need to face.

The only possible form of defence is transparent and authentic communication. Your organisation may not be the target of

---

4   Wikileaks: wikileaks.org
5   Collateral Murder, Wikileaks www.collateralmurder.com
6   Secret US Embassy Cables, Wikileaks: wikileaks.org/cablegate.html

Wikileaks, but Google provides consumers with access to the sum of all knowledge on the Internet. Social networks such as Facebook, Google+ and Twitter enable information to be shared and scrutinised with friends and colleagues. Companies must respect their relationships with their audiences. They must be transparent and avoid spin as customers who lose trust in a company or its products will be quick to go elsewhere. An organisation that attempts to be anything but completely honest is quickly shamed via social media. A claim made by a company about its international policy in London can be quickly verified across a network with people on the ground in Bombay, Mexico City or Sydney.

Pick a story on the other side of the world that has broken in today's news and try asking your network on Facebook, Google+ or Twitter to connect with someone involved in the breaking news and see how quickly you can get commentary on the story. We've tested this thesis on numerous occasions and it rarely takes more than 60 minutes before you're corresponding with someone local to the situation. In fact, news-gathering organisations apply this tactic to connect with individuals to get first-hand reports. During the aftermath of the earthquake in Japan in 2011, we exchanged messages on Twitter with people involved in a bid to test the veracity of international media reports. We quickly discovered flaws in the news reporting by news organisations that weren't on the ground.

Brandjacking: do you know who I am?

Occasionally, as journalists, we'd vent our fury at poor service by threatening to write a damning piece of editorial to shame an offending company into action. 'Do you know who I am?' was our childlike mantra. Only the most professional of journalists have not tried this tactic. Now, sitting on the receiving end of demands from the media, we're well used to the tactic. But 'Do you know who I am?' is no longer purely the refrain of journalists. Anyone with a blog or significant Twitter presence can call an organisation to account. The audience is answering back. Quentin Langley, the editor of a popular blog called Brandjack News[7], calls the ability for an individual to criticise and publically shame a company 'brandjacking' and, for now at least, it places the brand in a hostile relationship with the consumer.

TIME magazine showed incredible foresight when it named 'You' as the *TIME* Person of the Year in 2006[8]. The Internet means we're all important and can ask 'Do you know who I am?' of a company. An unhappy consumer has a platform through social media to voice their discontent and if it resonates with their social network it will be shared, amplifying the message. In July 2009, Canadian singer Dave Carroll became an overnight YouTube hit when he posted a song, 'United Breaks Guitars'[9], after his guitar was damaged at Chicago's O'Hare airport. He wrote the song after watching his guitar being thrown into the aircraft by baggage handlers and spent the following 12 months attempting to get compensation from United Airlines. The video had four million views in 10 days and United's share price fell by 10 per cent. It was a harsh wake-up call for corporations. In 2011 examples occurred on a weekly, if not daily, basis.

'Brands have always been careful of powerful customers. If you've got Henry Kissinger or Bill Clinton flying with you as a

7 Brandjack News: www.brandjacknews.com
8 TIME Magazine Person of the Year 2006 – You, TIME: www.time.com/time/specials/packages/0,28757,2019341,00.html
9 United Breaks Guitars, YouTube: www.youtube.com/watch?v=5YGc4zOqozo

customer, you have to be really careful. Because you know they can hurt you. But now anyone with access to the Internet can create and distribute content. If it resonates with your community online you have the potential to hurt a brand and you don't necessarily even have to be right,' says Langley.

Powerful individuals and journalists have always had the power and the platform to fight back but social media gives everyone a voice. But it is Langley's final point that strikes at the operation of the corporate communications department as the frontline defender of corporate reputation. Social media and networks have little regard for journalistic rigour or media law.

Authentic communication

In 1984, James E. Grunig and Todd Hunt published the Four Models of Public Relations as part of their book *Managing Public Relations*[10]. The model describes the different forms of communication between an organisation and its stakeholders. The first model is publicity or press agent, the second is known as the public relations information model, the third asymmetric persuasion, and the final one — the two-way symmetrical model — has become accepted as a formal definition of communication. It remains as relevant today for the era of digitised communication as it was when it was first created. Few organisations truly engage with their audiences as Grunig and Hunt describe, but are locked into one-way forms of communication. To return to Sheldrake's Six Influence Flows, they broadcast to their audience, focusing purely on the first flow of influence.

---

10 Grunig, James E, and Hunt, Todd. *Managing Public Relations*. Harcourt Brace Jovanovich College Publishers, 1984.

Model Name	Type of Communication	Characteristics
Press agent / publicity	One-way communication	Uses persuasion and manipulation to influence audiences to behave as the organisation desires.
Public information model	One-way communication	Uses press releases and other one-way communication techniques to distribute organisational information. The public relations practitioner is often referred to as the in-house journalist.
Two-way asymmetrical model	Two-way communication (imbalanced)	Uses persuasion and manipulation to influence audiences to behave as the organisation desires. Does not use research to find out how stakeholders feel about the organisation.
Two-way symmetrical model	Two-way communication	Uses communication to negotiate with the public, resolve conflict and promote mutual understanding and respect between the organisation and its stakeholders.

Table: James E. Grunig and Todd Hunt's Four Models of Public Relations

Propaganda relations

While technological change allows organisations to engage directly with their audiences, very few are actually doing so. Pick a consumer brand you admire and head to Facebook or Twitter and look up whether it has an account. It almost certainly will. But is it using that account to engage with its customers and prospects? More than likely it will be using its social media accounts to push out branded content as an extension of its web marketing efforts with little effort to engage. We exclude media owners from this exercise that use networks as an extension of their distribution network. It's early days but, to use Grunig and Hunt's model, corporate communicators remain wedded to propaganda relations as their primary means of communication.

In a paper published in the *PRism Journal* called 'Paradigms of global public relations in an age of digitalisation'[11], Grunig claims that organisations have embraced social media and networking as a knee-jerk reaction with little thought to how they use it as a strategic means of communication. It is no smarter than propaganda as a means of engagement. 'For most practitioners, digital media [changes] everything about the way they practise public relations. Other practitioners, however, doggedly use the new media in the same way as traditional media. From a theoretical perspective [...] I do not believe digital media change the public relations theory needed to guide practice, especially our generic principles of public relations. Rather, the new media facilitate the application of the principles and, in future, will make it difficult for practitioners around the world not to use the principles,' says Grunig.

Edward Bernays is credited as one of the forefathers of the public relations industry who understood the value of advocacy and direct audience engagement. His techniques are as relevant today as they were almost 100 years ago. One of Bernays's early campaigns saw him survey doctors and report their recommendation for consumers to eat a good breakfast to

---

11 Grunig, James E., University of Maryland. 'Paradigms of global public relations in an age of digitalisation'. *Prism Journal*, 2009.

improve their wellbeing. He sent the results to 5,000 doctors along with materials promoting eggs and bacon as a hearty breakfast. Sales of bacon inevitably rocketed as a result of his advocacy. Influenced undoubtedly by his uncle, Sigmund Freud, Bernays recognised that the public could be influenced in their thinking through advocacy or propaganda, as he wrote in his book, *Propaganda*, published in 1928[12]. Bernays was one of the first to spot the opportunity for a new industry that he called 'propaganda relations' which would use advocacy as a means of building influence, as opposed to the emergent advertising industry, which sought to buy attention. He quickly, and in hindsight wisely, renamed this business public relations as a result of the negative connotations associated with propaganda during World War II.

Bernays worked for US President Woodrow Wilson during World War I, forming the Committee on Public Information to influence US public opinion towards supporting US participation in the war. He was responsible for devising the campaign spearheaded by the slogan 'bringing democracy to Europe'. In 1919, he was invited by Wilson to attend the Paris Peace Conference, a meeting of the Allied victors, to set the peace terms for Germany and other opposition forces. Bernays was stunned by the level of support for the United States and the degree to which his democracy slogan had taken root. That same year, Bernays opened a public relations agency in New York and developed his craft. Many of his campaigns and tactics would be familiar to anyone working in a public relations agency today. Arguably his most effective piece of work was the promotion of tobacco to women on behalf of the American Tobacco Company. Prior to 1920, smoking amongst women was

---

12 Bernays, Edward. *Propaganda*. I G Publishing, 1928.

taboo. Bernays' solution was to persuade debutantes to smoke in the 1929 Easter Day Parade as an act of defiance against male-dominated society. He succeeded in creating a news event that was reported by journalists and photographers across the United States. The campaign made it socially acceptable for women to smoke. But more than that, it created the perception that it was *cool* for young women to smoke, and opened up a new and lucrative audience for the tobacco business where advertising had previously failed.

The corporate obsession with press releases and other wire fodder

Ivy Lee was another early pioneer of the public relations industry. He was the founder of a New York public relations firm in 1905. Twelve months later, he sent the world's first press release as part of a crisis communication effort on behalf of the Pennsylvania Railroad. He persuaded the railroad company to issue a press release after an electric train fell off a drawbridge; 53 people were killed. Lee's intention was to engage openly with media organisations and, on the basis that rumours quickly fill a void in communication, get a statement directly to journalists before other versions of the story could be spread. It was a strategy that worked. The *New York Times* printed the press release the following day word-for-word as a statement from the railroad.

The tactics may have changed but Lee's response of communicating quickly and openly in a crisis situation is as appropriate today as it was more than 100 years ago. Despite huge advances in technology, the press release remains one of the primary forms of communication between an organisation and journalists. Proponents of social networking get excited about an organisation's potential to communicate directly with its audiences but, in the main, organisations remain wedded to the press release as a means of communication. They have mangled its purpose to communicate not only with journalists but other audiences, such as analysts and customers. The modern-day press release – with its familiar format of a date line, headline, body content and boilerplate – remains unchanged.

Here's a challenge. Head to one of the wire services such as Businesswire or Marketwire and check the headlines of the first 50 press releases. How many contain news? By news, we mean a story that would satisfy news-gathering criterion set out by the Associated Press or Thomson Reuters, and would lead a journalist to follow up on the press release and write up a story. Here's the reality; the majority of press releases do not contain news content. The press release has become a general purpose document that an organisation publishes on its website and issues via a wire service, not to inform the media of a news event, but typically to reach broader audiences and to satisfy an internal audience. It's a catch-all communication tactic that seeks to address Sheldrake's multiple influence flows around an organisation rather than purely external audiences. We call them wire fodder or public relations spam.

PR spam

The issue of public relations spam has come into sharp focus in the public relations industry in the last five years. It has been exacerbated by technology. Commercial media databases enable untrained public relations executives to create email lists of hundreds of journalists and push out irrelevant content at the push of a button. Adding another 100 or even 200 names to a distribution list, just in case a press release might be relevant, is trivial. When asked to provide the size of a typical distribution list the media database firms we contacted were all reluctant to provide a figure.

In a future where reputation is governed by the strength of your network and your relationship with your audience, databases break a basic rule of network theory by providing individuals with a shortcut into the network. The flaw in this model was apparent long before the arrival of social media.

Dan Ilett[13] is a journalist-turned-media entrepreneur who knows only too well about this issue, and claims that it has got so bad that it's getting in the way of journalists doing their job. During his career, Ilett has written for some of the leading newspapers and business magazines in Europe, including the *Financial Times* and *The Economist* Group. Most recently, he founded the environmental business website Greenbang. On a good day he says that he receives 30 to 40 press releases and pitches, rising to hundreds on a bad day.

'I divert press releases into a folder and scan the headlines once a day. The majority are ignored and deleted because the headline is so badly written. In any other business it would be classed as spam,' says Ilett. 'With any other business communication, you have an option to opt out or receive information the way you prefer. It's permission-based. Not with PRs. They abuse email and jam their nasty little press releases in your inbox so you have more work to do. The answer to all this – as it always will be – is good headline writing. Get to the point. Twitter and text messages force you to do that,' he says.

Journalists are fighting back and starting to put controls in place against public relations spam. Twitter provides a brutal means of managing public relations professionals and it's no surprise that journalists are increasingly insisting that PRs use Twitter as the primary means of pitching a story. It puts the journalist back in control of the relationship. By using Twitter,

13 Dan Ilet's personal website: www.danilett.com

journalists can block or choose not to follow anyone that consistently pitches poor content. Shortmail is another tool that journalists are starting to use to cut their inboxes down to size. It's an email system that is limited to 500 characters of text and is accessible to anyone who wants to read it. The brevity and transparency may just force the public relations industry to do a better job.

Ilett claims that the majority of pitches and press releases are pushed out by individuals that don't understand the subject matter, let alone the audience. Yet the pressure on journalists to file copy accurately and quickly has never been more acute but, according to Ilett, the content being promoted by the public relations industry is getting worse. 'Trust is becoming a vital currency in the relationship between journalists and their sources. I have a small number of PRs that I work with whom I trust to pitch my story. Beyond that, I get my information elsewhere and within a corporate organisation that's typically from executives who are creating the stories rather than the corporate communicators that are dressing them up as public relations fodder,' says Ilett.

An Inconvenient PR Truth

UK-based wire service, Realwire, claims that a mammoth 1.7 billion irrelevant press release emails are received each year by UK and US journalists. It led a campaign called an Inconvenient PR Truth in 2010 to raise awareness of the issue. It worked with the Chartered Institute of Public Relations (CIPR), the Public Relations Consultants Association (PRCA), the Investor Relations Society (IRS) and the National Union of Journalists (NUJ) on a spamming charter and crowd-sourced a so-called Bill of Rights for the public relations industry. These documents set out a minimum set of standards for PR's communication with journalists. Despite widespread consultation, it has been largely ignored. Occasionally, journalists bite back and publish lists of offenders, but largely the issue goes on unchecked because database providers and wire services have no interest in cannibalising their own market.

Realwire CEO, Adam Parker, believes that it's because the public relations industry, unlike other professional service industries such as the accountancy or legal professions, has no imperative to change. 'Regulation forces education and seeks to stamp out bad practice in other industries. The lack of regulation in the public relations industry means there is no necessity for those purveyors of bad practice to take action, and such practitioners are also unlikely to take much notice of standards initiatives from professional bodies such as the CIPR and the PRCA,' says Parker.

Parker's solution to the issue of spam is technology-driven. Like Ilett he has little confidence in education in the public relations industry. Realwire is making a lone bid to tackle the issue with a service called PR Filter[14]. It's an open, web-based platform that puts users, in this case bloggers and journalists, back in control. The web application scans a blogger's or journalist's online output for the past six months and serves up press release content from the major wire services based on their areas of interest. There are three variables to broaden or reduce the number of results: relevance (low to high), time (how far back you want to extend a search) and geography (source of content). Its simplicity belies the massive amount of computing power required to semantically analyse the 15,000 press releases handled by the platform each week.

PR Filter has proved that a software application is capable of automatically profiling the interests of thousands of recipients

---

14 Realwire's PR Filter: prfilter.com

and then match thousands of releases a day to those recipients, at a level of relevance that feedback suggests is significantly better that that achieved by current distribution services. In fact, in many cases significantly better than that achieved by many individual public relations practitioners. But uptake is slow, admits Parker. 'The success of PR Filter or services like it depends on the public relations and media communities adopting and supporting such a tool. It's a similar issue to the one that Spotify faces. It is trying to solve the problem of illegal downloads through balancing the interests of music creator publishers with consumers. However, it will only do so if consumers adopt and support its model. Anyone trying to implement such a service is therefore faced with a similar challenge to Spotify to try and encourage the relevant communities to engage and support it,' he says.

The future of communication flows between an organisation and its audiences will continue to remain in flux for some time. But overcoming the issue of irrelevant content or public relations spam is an issue that the public relations industry must tackle if it is to remain relevant and have a role in organisational communication. If not a technical solutions such as PR Filter will allow recipients to proactively take control of the content that they receive.

Searching for answers

We have explored how the press release has been abused by the public relations industry but it's not the only offender. The online search industry has recognised the opportunity that press releases and wire services offer to build inbound links as a tactic to improve keyword search rankings. Faux news content is distributed via a wire service with the goal of securing widespread coverage around target keywords and web links on editorially driven websites that are ranked highly by search engines such as Google and Yahoo.

It's a crude tactic that has been proven to be flawed but it still goes on according to Kelvin Newman, creative director of UK search engine, SiteVisibility, and producer of the Internet Marketing podcast[15]. 'Press release syndication never has, and never will, be an essential element to a search link-building campaign. Optimising press releases for keywords is about low hanging fruit. If they are going online, you're mad not to be giving them the once over for keywords, but I doubt many link builders would be upset if they lost the ability to syndicate press releases,' he says.

Not only is it a flawed strategy but it can also create confusion and result in reputational damage. In a major update to its search algorithm called Panda[16] in the first half of 2011, Google took action against sites that consisted of low-quality content and organisations that had a high search ranking as a result of large chunks of content being replicated around the Internet. US retailer, JC Penney, was one of the casualties of Google's action. It previously ranked highly across a range of keywords for consumer products. In many instances JC Penney had a higher search ranking than the manufacturers of the products that it sold.

The media despise the tactic of spraying out content to media websites. Nick Davies coined the term 'churnalism' in his book *Flat Earth News*[17] to describe how the media, under pressure to file content to the web, is distorted by public relations-driven propaganda. 'This is the heart of modern journalism, the rapid

15 Internet Marketing podcast: www.sitevisibility.co.uk/impodcast/

16 Finding more high-quality sites in search, Google Blog: http://googleblog. blogspot.com/2011/02/finding-more-high-quality-sites-in.html

17 Davis, Nick. *Flat Earth News.* Chatto & Windus, 2008.

repackaging of largely unchecked second-hand material, much of it designed to service the political or commercial interests of those who provide it... This is why researchers from Cardiff University [who investigated this issue] found that, among even the best national papers in the country, only 12 per cent of their stories were their own work and only 12 per cent of key facts were being checked.'

The Media Standards Trust, a UK-based charity that promotes standards in journalism, operates a website called Churnalism. com. It enables visitors to paste chunks of content into a churn engine, which compares the text against a constantly updated database of articles from UK media outlets. The results show the percentage of any given article that has been reproduced from public relations material. For example, a survey about television catchphrases on behalf of OnePoll.com was published almost verbatim by *The Sun*[18], the *Daily Mirror*[19] and the *Daily Telegraph*[20] in January 2010. It paints a dismal picture for the future of original reporting and fact-checking in the UK media.

We return again to the issue of authenticity and transparency. Search marketing techniques are developing as fast as search algorithms and attempts to dupe search engines will always be penalised. But good online public relations aimed at connecting an organisation using interesting and meaningful content will

---

18 Yeah, but Vicky has best telly phrase, *The Sun*: www.thesun.co.uk/sol/homepage/showbiz/tv/2824188/Vicky-Pollard-has-best-TV-comedy-catchphrase.html

19 Little Britain's Vicky Pollard has funniest catchphrase, the *Daily Mirror*: www.mirror.co.uk/tv-entertainment/most-popular/2010/01/26/little-britain-s-vicky-pollard-has-funniest-catchphrase-115875-21995626/

20 Little Britain's Vicky Pollard takes catchphrase crown for 'yeah but no but yeah', the *Daily Telegraph*: www.telegraph.co.uk/culture/tvandradio/7070986/Little-Britains-Vicky-Pollard-takes-catchphrase-crown-for-yeah-but-no-but-yeah.html

always be rewarded by search rankings. By all means optimise the content of a press release for search marketing once it has been drafted but don't have search marketing as your primary objective.

Press release distribution is a small sideshow in the debate about the differences between the public relations and search marketing industries. In truth, the public relations industry was slow to spot the opportunity presented by the online search and missed the chance to broaden its offer. That oversight has cost the public relations industry dearly. Econsultancy, a community for digital marketing and ecommerce professionals[21], estimated that the natural search marketing industry in the UK grew by 16 per cent in 2010, reaching a value of £436 million, up from £376 million in 2009. This represents approximately 12 per cent of the value of the total UK search engine marketing sector last year, which Econsultancy estimates to have been worth £3.63 billion. The scale of the US market is even more staggering. It rose to $16.6 billion in 2010, according to Econsultancy. The debate about whether public relations or search agencies are best placed to deliver search marketing campaigns has been well and truly won by the search industry but there have been plenty of scraps along the way and there will inevitably be more to come.

The social media press release

The first attempt to redefine the format of the press release since Ivy Lee devised it in 1906 came with the advent of the social web. Public relations practitioners debated with journalists via blogs how the text format could be enhanced to

---

21 Econsultancy Search marketing stats roundup, Econsultancy Blog: econsultancy.com/uk/blog/7580-search-marketing-stats-round-up-2

incorporate hyperlinks, images, audio and video. Todd Defren, Principal at SHIFT Communications based in Boston, Massachusetts, created a social media news release template[22] that was quickly adopted by the public relations industry. Subsequent revisions have added social functions such as Facebook 'like' and Twitter sharing.

Just as the media has fragmented, so too has the process of corporate communication. Press releases are as likely to turn up in search results, shared on Facebook or Twitter, or published on a blog, as they are to be used as a means of communicating with traditional media audiences. Using the web to add richer content beyond text and hyperlinks adds context and makes a traditionally dry document more interesting and likely to be shared by its audience. It provides a means to link to relevant areas of your own site or third-party sites and allows content to shared and commented upon.

The simplest way to create a social media press release is to use a blogging platform such as Wordpress to create your own documents and append them to your web presence. Bespoke social media newsrooms can be incorporated into any corporate website and wire distribution providers have been quick to build social media news release distribution into their services. The social media release may be built to enable an organisation to share its content with journalists and bloggers, but that is the limitation of its social features. But it is not remotely social in the sense of providing a mechanism for the audience to engage and answer back. The primary purpose of the press release – a means of broadcasting communication from an organisation out to its audiences – remains exactly the same as when Lee

---

22 Social Media News Release, SHIFT Communications: www.shiftcomm. com/downloads/smprtemplate.pdf

sent the first press release about the Pennsylvania Railroad crash one hundred years ago.

Authenticity is crucial to the success of organisational communications. Operating in the modern media environment is tough — there's no doubt about that. You need a clear and distinct strategy to tell and sustain the interest in a story over a period of time, and messages must be seamless and transparent across all channels. You also need to integrate communications across all areas of your business, from customer relations to sales, and you must be ready for when the audience answers back and moves towards a strategy of engagement and participation.

Summary

- The fragmentation of media resulting from the development of the Internet means that it is no longer possible for an organisation to dominate the news agenda.
- The Internet enables an organisation to monitor the flows of influence between itself and its stakeholders, and vice versa. Similarly flows of communication between an organisations' competitors and its stakeholders can be monitored.
- Social media democratises communication and gives everyone the opportunity to have a voice online. It enables organisations to communicate directly with their audiences.
- Attempts to mechanise media relations are flawed. The majority of press releases contain no news content and media databases shortcut the process of building relationships to the annoyance of journalists.
- Search marketing strategies that attempt to dupe search engine algorithms will always be penalised. As with public relationship authenticity is crucial to long-term success.

CHAPTER

5

THE AUDIENCE ANSWERS BACK

Brands are being baited. Brands are under an intense spotlight. Their audiences want to talk. Is it even optional? #brandanarchy

When two, now former, employees appeared on YouTube, apparently stuffing cheese up their nostrils and farting on sausages when preparing food, Domino's Pizza[1] soon realised that everyone in an organisation is now a spokesperson.

Well, not really a spokesperson, but certainly a public representative of the organisation, and a publisher. So, is social networking a communications anarchy that can deflate or implicate a brand at the touch of a keyboard, leaving organisations at the whim of a mobilised army of on-payroll publishers? Well, we've always had the ability to publish. A person who puts something on a village green noticeboard is a publisher, and is subject to all of the same legalities, at least in England and Wales.

Everyone working for a brand can be its spokesperson. That has always been the case. But with social media, everyone else can now be a brand analyst in a matter of seconds.

Of course, most brands have a relatively limited number of authorised spokespeople who speak on its behalf via the conventional media. Their content delivery is typically well planned, structured and engineered to develop reputation in the right direction, at the right time. However, there are also

---

1 Domino's Pizza Employee fired and arrested (CNBC): www.youtube.com/watch?v=ZtjVEBZWweM&feature=related

renegade unauthorised spokespeople, normally aggrieved 'company insiders' who leak information to the press or who make claims about their employers in some other public forum. Typically though, by their nature, these cause short-lived problems.

What many brands rarely consider, though, is that lots of their employees interface with the conventional media in other ways: phoning in reports on their son's rugby team to the local paper, publicising a charity bike ride in a personal capacity but referencing their employer in doing so, writing to the editor of a newspaper about the council's failure to collect the bins on time – accompanied by a follow-up 'angry resident' picture story the following week. Some can have a positive impact on reputation, some can be negative, most are neutral. Just because authorised spokespeople are subject to controls does not mean that a brand's engagement with audiences through the conventional media is ever really controlled. Employment contracts can help, but are a deterrent rather than a gag, and can be unenforceable anyway. It is just that there is some reasonable degree of influence over the influence, and therefore reputation.

So the unfortunate scenes at Domino's spotlighted an acute organisational risk. One of the changes they highlighted was that people can now publish at will, and so drag a brand down with a few clicks of a mouse. The bigger change though was that everyone in the world may now be watching. And those people watching also now have the ability – and often the willingness – to answer back.

Particularly if bad things are being done to pizzas.

What was largely a one-way street is now a two-way street. The information superhighway goes in both directions, so editorial influence on reputation is faster and complex.

Why are we baiting?

Again, control would seem to be slipping out of the hands of brands. The ability for consumers to respond to external communications by a brand, or even instigate discussion, places a burden of expectation on brands to engage in conversation, or risk looking dismissive. And, as we have said repeatedly, the entire world could be watching.

A conversation that begins between a brand and a consumer, who is probably a customer, can escalate in minutes to involve comments, viewpoints, allegations or irrelevance from thousands of others across continents. With millions looking on.

The worst thing brand managers can do is panic, or bury their heads in the sand. It is not enough for them to go wobbly-kneed at the *what*, they must also investigate the *why* – why audiences choose to engage with a brand using social media, and what they're looking to get out of doing so. And is what those audiences contribute to social media really a true reflection of how they perceive the brand? Perhaps most importantly, have they always felt this way about the brand, always influenced its perception by word-of-mouth and always actually wanted to engage with it in some way?

If the latter is true, social media can be far more of an opportunity than a threat.

Getting to grips with that requires many questions to be answered. While it's not the central issue, one very important part of all this is the question of why anyone would want to bait a brand into a 'bad' conversation in the first place? A big factor though, obviously, is the brand in question.

Yet it is not just what you are, it's what you do – or don't do. Conventional media's bad-guy brands are obvious – those most likely to get a bad rap, or at least may start off on the back foot as far as reputation is concerned, are the most overt capitalists – oil companies, mining firms, energy providers and the like

– and those large multinationals that face big cost pressures to be competitive – retailers, airlines, telecoms firms, the food and drinks industry, and so on. Social media's publishers, readers and analysers may have the same preconceptions, but in today's multi-way media world it is behaviour that invariably has the largest single impact on a brand's reputation.

'Oh behave!'

Brand behaviour? Before social media, that phrase was most likely to have been uttered in the context of whether a brand was being 'good' or whether it was demonstrating that it was 'behaving itself'. A playground-like notion born of expectations of corporate responsibility, citizenship and plain old common sense. Has social media changed that? Well, those expectations still exist, and some might argue they have been heightened by social media's glare and immediacy. But really, the change is that digitised, networked conversation has added an extra dimension. It is that of how a brand responds to criticism or questions about its market and activities, and whether indeed the brand is inspiring, demonstrates leadership or even, where appropriate, is amusing when it starts a conversation in the first place.

Part of the fear factor that many brands harbour about participating in social media conversations is that they aren't the ones starting those conversations about themselves. Regardless, such conversations are going on all around us, and can be more influential than a brand's own communication. Customers, broader consumers, industry watchers and those with an axe to grind – think union members in the case of a workplace dispute – are not just willing to get involved in the chat, they're actively seeking it. They're thriving on it. They want to tell tales about your brand and provide their own perspectives.

Secondly, the social media audience's appetite for these stories – those begun by a lone individual or, using appropriate behaviour, by the brand itself – is becoming ravenous. Individuals are increasingly realising that their brand choices can influence corporate performance, and that expressing their views can swing political fortunes. They've realised what can be achieved by harnessing the power of inspirational digitised conversation. Each wallet can wield a very small amount of power over a brand, but many wallets can make or break it, and social media too has that unifying influence. Reputation is, implicitly, at the heart of every online conversation about a brand or the markets in which it is active. Given this shift in the nature of a brand's relationship with its audiences, largely driven by the ability to answer back, and the associated additional expectations for brand behaviour, the priorities for today's brands are being stretched well beyond being there to make money for shareholders. The new priorities extend beyond shareholders to stakeholders – customers, employees, investors, partners and the environment.

Which at least helps set out the scope of conversations that brands need to engage in, and provides some steer on what type of brand behaviour is expected by those audiences. And once brands are clear on those factors, they are on their way to being able to use social media to their advantage. They can gain the ability to have a degree of command over their reputation by influencing the editorial content about their brand and its circulation online – because they are set up to create and nurture conversation, rather than just participate in it or nod from the fringes.

In those conversations, brands must be bold. To be assured about how bold brands can be, and that their reputations can be enhanced or at least maintained through their participation, what they say and how they do it must be both appropriate and in context. By being appropriate and having a real understanding of, from the stakeholder's perspective, the context when they engage in conversation, they can ensure that they're not turned upon. Or simply ignored.

That way, it doesn't matter if brands are baited; they will get baited anyway. By being able to engage boldly in conversations about themselves – and indeed beyond – they can stand up for themselves and make a stand that builds positive reputation, in a world of changed behavioural expectations.

The social media bear pit

In the real world, not all conversations are joyous. Quite clearly, they aren't all a bundle of laughs in social media either, which is probably one of the main reasons why you've read this far.

So you have thought long and hard about how your brand can best engage in conversations. You know you can be bold, you know you can exude the most appropriate behaviour. You've monitored anything and everything online about your brand and its markets. In just the same way as you would when having a conversation in a pub or bar, you've drawn breath. You've looked around at your audience. You've prepared your opening line.

Time to jump in. To jump into what could well be, or quickly become, a public slanging match around the brand. A conversation that spirals perilously out of control. With an exchange of comments, information and materials that make you wonder why you bothered, and whether you'll be able to stand up for yourself.

Looking at some of the snippets of those so-called conversations, you might be forgiven for thinking that social media is more like a kangaroo court, an exercise in political philandering or a loose-knit ensemble of highly vocal people realising they have a new-found power.

That is largely because the most extreme, most potent, most pungent social media conversations are those which tend to end up at the forefront of brands' attention. Rightly so, given that they are likely to be amongst those with the greatest negative influence on reputation. But the same is absolutely true of editorial content published in conventional media. And, at the risk of making a simplistic point, of life writ large: you never know what's going to be thrown at you.

How can brands have confidence that they're ready for anything when they dive into social media conversations? Well, they can never be completely sure, but the same is true of conventional media, and indeed any other situation that a business may face. What you can do is do your best to understand who you're conversing with and what the rules of engagement are, particularly when things get a little rough.

We've already looked at what is required to identify and understand the audience. So, looking next at the rules of engagement, the first is the most crucial: brands must be transparent, so the onus is on them to be both honest and clear. If they seek to bend the facts or change the tune, they'll be found out because digitised conversations leave an audit trail and anyone could be watching closely. If they're opaque, brands' behaviour may be pilloried and their messages may be distorted.

Transparency forces honesty and clarity. Brands have had to move to a more transparent relationship with the customers since Internet access became mainstream and customers were able to gain more information about them. Now they are being compelled to do the equivalent of conversing directly with any and all stakeholders while the world records the conversation, then plays it back and critiques it. In time, brands will come to realise that this is a good thing; that if they can get involved in the right conversation and drive editorial influence through the content that transpires, they have far more to gain than they have to lose. But it still requires a shift in mindset and marketing approach, compared to the way that brands have built and maintained their reputations in the past. Whereas those actively contributing to social media conversations on behalf of a brand today tend to be either digital media enthusiasts or spokespeople sanctioned to carry out the role, in the future it is entirely feasible that everyone within an organisation may have to do so. They will all have to be accustomed to being a public 'face' of the brand and rather than a small number of people being authorised as spokespeople, it will be a necessary core skill for all worker, much like having to represent the organisation every time they pick up the phone.

When conversation takes flight

Just like those real, verbal conversations, social media spokespeople need sufficient free reign to be able to deviate, within acceptable bounds, from the corporate script in order to achieve their aims. Just as sales and customer service personnel are trained to be, for example, gracious and acknowledging in the face of customer criticism, so must conversations in social media be both transparent and honest when a brand or its activities are criticised. Ultimately, if you're wrong you must admit it; if you disagree you must agree to disagree; and if you're blindingly brilliant at something, or have been proven right at the expenses of others, there's a commonsense need to show a bit of humility. In digitised conversations, as in real conversations, it is not just what you say, but how and when you say it. And a little grown-up grace can go a long way.

Similarly, humour has to be approached cautiously. You have to know your audience: you wouldn't blunder into a group conversation in a pub cracking cheap gags about something sensitive like weight loss only to find out that half the group had eating disorders that had taken them to the brink of severe depression. Likewise, you must think hard about trying to be funny in a social media conversation, and appreciate that many more people are listening and their personal viewpoints are therefore likely to vary widely. What seems a tepid joke in one part of the world can be highly offensive in another, and the conversation may take the ugliest of turns. Politics, sex and religion can make very amusing conversation topics, but only providing you know exactly how the recipient of the joke will react. Equally, there are many safe-bet topics, such as sport and the weather, that are pretty much fair game anywhere; so the light touch of humour can humanise a brand to the benefit of its reputation.

Finally, there is an obvious rule of conversation that must be respected in social media – no one loves a loudmouth. You may get heard by everyone, but you will not grow in their estimation if your communication resorts to shouting louder and more frequently than everyone else. For many brands, simply speaking up once or twice in a fairly difficult conversation can be enough to answer criticism and gain respect.

With all elements of social media conversations, drawing a parallel with appropriate behaviour in real-world conversations is the best starting point, and will avoid most of the pitfalls. Which is why those conversations that brands get dragged into against their will, in which they are practically teased into responding to, may be particularly dangerous.

You're being watched, everywhere

There is no doubt that brands are being goaded into responding to social media. Unlike the case with conventional media, in the world of social media brands cannot just take the risk of declining an interview or making excuses about a packed diary making talk-time impossible. If they don't respond, it can be like a guilty plea being entered in their absence.

But while responses must be appropriate and relatively rapid, they must also be issued with a clear comprehension of what impact that content will have on their reputations and how it may be published across many different media platforms. There are the classic, well-commanded examples of a social media exercise – for instance an amusing or engaging video put on YouTube – that create much conversation and interest across other social media, to the extent that they gets picked up by conventional media and, before you know it, are featured on the evening television news. By 'picked up', we of course mean picked up following an appropriate steer from a public relations agency paid to plug the brand and build its reputation. But the ability of content to be passed as-is from one type of media to another, or filtered into something that makes it more appropriate for the media in question, is increasingly commonplace. As media converges and, in the example of *The Guardian* newspaper's website, a publisher begins to push reader engagement and experience on multiple fronts in relation to the same topic, content does not so much evolve across different platforms but is available from a number of appropriate sources at the same time. That way, the reader is given the option to read or respond to the content how they want to.

Regardless of dissemination points though, the important factor here is how quickly the audience for content can grow, and how something intended for a relatively niche group can, unless you're shrewd and plan for such outcomes, end up in the faces of millions. It is best to assume that anyone and everyone may end up seeing your content, so it is essential that this is factored into your communication planning, and that the domino effect of cross-media momentum is used to your advantage, where appropriate. Content that may not get much interest if you aim it at broad-brush media may be better targeted at a respected special interest journal, at least initially — think of the *New Scientist*, for example. Once that journal touts its story via Twitter, your brand can pick up the reins and push it further, so much so that the likes of the BBC picks it up and covers it across radio and TV news bulletins, with more in-depth analysis online. Bingo.

Conversation is also complex

Yet let's not get lulled into thinking that conventional media is all one-way and social media offers the only scope for conversations. Yes, *The Guardian* is a prime example of media that offers multiple content types, but many online publishers now offer the ability for readers to put their views across in the form of comment streams, feedback columns, Facebook fan pages and links to follow the brand on Twitter. Comment streams are particularly powerful, given that they are a good way for a publisher to develop a story editorially with relevant input from readers – a smart brand can say the right things in comment streams so that it influences the total editorial in its favour, in a way that's there for all to see when the piece gets disseminated across social media. Nous is needed to make this work well, though: too much blatant publicity-mongering and the comment will get vetoed by editorial controllers; too little, and your point will be lost on the audience.

It is a powerful example, however, of how a little editorial intervention in the right place at the right time can help to steer the right kind of exposure, and influence the reputation of the brand. Many social media novices say they don't know where to start – for many brand managers now engaged with social media, the bigger problem can be knowing where to stop.

Sustaining conversations across social media takes not only time, but editorial savvy and the authorisation to be engaged in the first place. While media has diversified beyond all prior comprehension in the past few years, and will ultimately have to consolidate, the challenge remains that there is simply too much ground to be covered for a brand to expect to be appropriately involved in every conversation that is relevant to it. Instead, brands must pick and choose those conversations that will have the greatest impact on reputation, as well as on customer service, employee engagement and corporate citizenship. There is no magic formula for doing this – as is the case with conventional media, facts must be gathered about the scope and audience of each media type, then the most valuable ones monitored for editorial output and engaged for editorial success.

Which takes people. Brand communication has long been overseen and implemented by a combination of internal teams and, where appropriate, outside agencies and contractors. This hierarchy has historically provided a resource for structured and responsive reputation management through conventional media and direct engagement channels. Social media does not fundamentally change that, but it does place an onus on those teams to develop new skills, understand how reputation management works across social media and assign responsibility to the right people.

The oft-lauded social media strategy has no place in this, because there really is no such thing. Did you ever have a local radio strategy? No, you just developed appropriate approaches to that media based on need, driven ultimately by commercial objectives. What matters is your business strategy – get that clear, and brand managers can then best plot reputation management across the entire media landscape; not just fret and pontificate over the brave new social world.

The worst thing your marketing team can do is form a digital division to handle the specific requirements of reputation management in social media. Creating expertise niches when the media is a cauldron of change is just asking for trouble in a world that requires transparency, agility, coordinated communication and the editorially sensitive delivery of content across all media. It is far better to develop a plan for ensuring that all brand managers understand all media, and that specific responsibilities are designated for certain media titles, communication programmes and initiatives. Many brands are not there yet, but as media alignment is typically the most effective structure for media engagement, this is not the time to be creating ghettos of social media haves and have-nots.

Does this fundamentally change the job of the modern brand manager, at least as far as external communication goes? Well, yes and no. Yes, in that more skills are required as roles will require greater sophistication, and brand communication will need to be closely aligned with – and in cases overlap with – the functions of customer relationship management and human resources. But no, in that many of the fundamentals of communicating with customers, prospects and other stakeholders remain the same. Brands must say the right things to the right people in the right way in order to meet their commercial objectives. They must be responsive when engaged by those audiences over two-way media channels. And, as has always been the case, they must prioritise in doing the things that will have the greatest impact on commercial outcomes.

The chatter that matters

So, how do you know which conversations will most impact upon brand reputation? A bit of bad news for astute communication planners working to routine cycles: you don't.

But a lot of the priorities can be set out in advance. It's just that digital conversations are like real ones, just on a much larger scale. They can take sudden twists and turns. They can fade away in the face of competition from new information or topics. They can rapidly lose momentum when individuals who've been driving them lose interest. They can suddenly be thrust into the spotlight to the amazement of all involved.

Is that really that different to the prioritisation challenges we've long faced in managing brand reputation across conventional media? Not really. Brands have always had to prioritise how they handle the conventional media that will be most influential for them, depending on the nature of their business. They've always had to prioritise how they develop, channel and amend content based largely on their commercial priorities and, let's be honest, the occasional whim or whiff of internal politics. The big change is the pace at which this stuff moves; how agile brands must be in order to shift gears through conversations and decide what action to take when their priorities and the directions of social media conversations change.

Armed with an integrated communication plan and a clear understanding of which media are likely to have most influence on reputation, brands must ideally instigate digital conversations as well as monitor those going on across all media, so that they can take decisions quickly and respond to situations as soon as they arise. It may be that they decide not to intervene or, alternatively, they might interject in an attempt to divert the conversation towards other content or another topic. It may be that it's a conversation they have to be at the heart of, or which centres squarely on them so that to ignore it would be damaging to brand reputation. Whatever the scenario, if brands cannot see or hear what's going on, or assess a conversation's relevance to their reputation, they are not in a strong position for determining the appropriate course of action.

Give a little, take a lot?

Just as with conventional media, brands cannot be expected to answer every question, and be available to everyone at the drop of a hat. But there is an expectation, and it is in their best interests, to be fully aware of the risks and rewards associated with what they choose to say and how they choose to behave.

It is much the same for deciding how to handle social media conversations or questions that affect other areas of a brand's operations. As mentioned briefly earlier, social media is changing the face of customer relationship management and human resources too. There is a growing expectation from customers that if your brand engages online in any way via social media, that is carte blanche for entirely transparent dialogue with the public. You're either engaged or you're not, just like it not being possible to be half-pregnant. Gone are the days of being able to keep customers at arm's length through centralised call centres with lengthy 'on hold' queues, with other contact points deliberately kept opaque. Instead, brands have to learn that customers will approach them using social media, and that the way they're handled can be visible to the whole world.

Employee engagement using social media is typically less structured (and in many cases has evolved organically), and is driven by individuals within the business who came to social media early. The watchword here is consistency – if you're saying one thing to customers in order to drive reputation but saying something else to staff, it will be immediately obvious. Instead, brands are realising that pointing their employees to the way that the brand is engaging with the wider world online is a highly effective way to keep them informed, aligned with brand messages and feeling a sense of engagement with the brand at large.

Like commonsense approaches to integrated marketing, brand communication should be undertaken with mutual understanding and clear visibility across reputation, customer relations and employee relations activities. Transparency and immediacy mean that there is no real alternative.

Summary

- Audiences are starting to bait brands into conversations that they may not want to have. Why is that, and what are the risks and opportunities?
- How brutal can those negative conversations get, and where can they lead?
- Remember that your brand exists in the minds of the audiences. By understanding them better and what influence their perceptions better, you can establish how best to improve your reputation.
- There is a new level of scrutiny being applied to brands online. Brands need to be able to work out how to make the most of that, rather than running scared.
- There is so much noise and talk online. How can brands work out what really matters to them?

CHAPTER

6

ON THE INSIDE

Is talk cheap or extremely valuable? And how do employers work out which things their staff say are really important, and learn from them? #brandanarchy

So media change has forced organisations to communicate differently because external audiences have greater ability to interact with, and scrutinise, brands than they did in the past. It has also forced organisations to look long and hard at how their own people are communicating with their colleagues.

The same technological advancements that have changed the nature of public media have empowered employees on the inside too. But handled appropriately, they can empower employers too.

To understand this, it's best to look back at how internal communications used to be planned, delivered and evaluated, and how digital tools can offer new possibilities today.

Firstly, it's a relatively young discipline, at least in the guise we think of today. It draws on influences and techniques from many other marketing and communications disciplines and, like public relations, is rooted in the study of psychology. While large organisations in particular have a lengthy history of orchestrating and promoting a sense of pride and unity amongst employees through specific activities or engrained philanthropic attitudes (highlighted by the enlightened approach of some Victorian industrialists, for example), internal communications as a distinct function is new to the party.

Company newsletters and memos were often ineffective or in direct conflict with messages encouraged by trade unions. Messages, and the inherent values they sought to nurture, were often driven by the unions and, where they're active, still can be. In other organisations though, over the past three or more decades, the value of well-run employee communications and relations has been increasingly appreciated.

The real driver of the steady formalisation of internal communications has not been understanding and appreciation though; it has been technological progress. The presence of the telephone in offices more than 100 years ago opened up new communications possibilities that began to alter human behaviour and dynamics. The widespread arrival of the fax machine in the 1980s made a dent in the telephone's dominance, but not much of one. It was not until the arrival of the Internet that internal communications took a gargantuan leap forward.

So in the pre-Internet age, when the lines of communication started to be redrawn, impact on how staff perceived the brand they worked for was largely due to attempts by senior management to communicate major events or decisions that affected the business or organisation. But there was always a broader impact on perception caused, depending on the nature and size of the brand, by the media outside.

Take, for example, a brand involved in contentious operations or a brand that 'enjoys' a high media profile because its products were very much part of the fabric of everyday life around the world – food and drink companies, fashion houses, motor vehicle manufacturers, nuclear power plant operators and high street retailers spring to mind. The coverage of the brand by the mainstream media would invariably impact brand reputation, and hence the perceptions of the brand's employees and their peer group. Those who worked for such brands would face typical questions or remarks from others when asked where they worked, and there was no getting away from that.

It was almost a dirty secret, something rarely talked about with senior personnel or in anything other than a flippant, or irreverent, way. The nature of the reputation that existed in the minds and on the lips of external observers looking in would rarely even be acknowledged internally, let alone become the subject of an interactive discussion between the senior team and the rest of the staff. Any communication that did take place was normally carried out without the benefit of any plan or structure; it was employed often whimsically or reactively to counter negative media coverage by telling 'the truth of the matter', through some hastily-prepared internal statements.

The problem was that even when internal communications provided a full and frank account of the truth of the matter, there was a high risk that employees wouldn't believe it anyway, given that the raising of such matters would be a bolt from the blue, rather than part of any sustained dialogue.

And that was the stuff that stuck in the mind. In the past, more structured and sustained endeavours to maintain a direct and empathetic line to staff through internal communications would typically amount largely to meetings involving as many people as feasible, the oft-read but much-mocked noticeboard memo and, by comparison with online tools, primitive means that were not a huge step forward from schoolroom antics where notes were passed between desks in class.

Computerisation of the workplace made a big difference, but more to the atmosphere of the office than to the ability of brands to communicate with staff or encourage healthy communication between employees. It began in earnest in the mid-1980s, but it was to be a decade or more before the arrival of email as a mainstream workplace tool – rather than a useful aside – began to change the way people could talk and listen to others using their keyboards during the working day.

These days, it is perhaps difficult to imagine the impact that email had in its early days in the workplace. Before that, most people had spent most of their time communicating with colleagues and external contacts overtly – their phone calls and conversations at desks could readily be overheard. Before that, in the era when most workplaces consisted of many individual offices rather than open plan areas, the situation lent itself to even less open internal communication. With the arrival of email, fact and opinion could be transmitted not just between colleagues and business contacts but between people generally such as friends, family and acquaintances. To an extent it didn't matter. Email offered a way to mimic, in a basic way, the power of conventional media – it had the potential to inform and entertain. It didn't have anything like the collective mass influence of social media. It didn't have anything like the editorial credibility of conventional media nor the breadth or focus of some of today's owned media. But it was a sharp and colourful glimpse of things to come.

Email was silent, apart from the tapping of keyboards or the stifled laughter when something amused. It put mass and individual instantaneous communications at the fingertips of what became the vast majority of office-based workers, and ultimately having an email address became as mainstream as having a telephone number. It was the beginning of a quiet revolution in how people communicated amongst themselves internally in a wholly different and, potentially, extremely powerful way. The problem was that most brand owners hadn't a single clue how to turn it into an aide to more effective internal communications, and some even tried to ban it. They missed a massive trick, because it was a watershed moment in internal communications.

So who's in charge now?

The ability of email to connect people in what could become one large, largely unchecked and fast-moving conversation, spooked many brands. There was concern at the time that not only would email see productivity dip but that its use as a gossip channel would make it a threat rather than an asset to commercial success. In a way, it was a predecessor of social media from an internal communications standpoint. It showed how people could, if appropriate and in their own way, by the collective power of a group's principles and interest, apply editorial controls to content that was circulating socially.

Today, the lines are blurring all over the place. With commentary in the conventional media about brands now also being rapidly circulated within companies via social media, it's easy to suggest that there are no longer any real barriers between internal and external media. To that extent, it's easy to conclude that brands see little or no hope of ever regaining even a shard of control over internal media.

There is no editorial gatekeeper, at least not in the way that there used to be. In many ways, given the speed at which content can be criticised, forwarded, embellished and debated internally using the Internet, the editorial gatekeeping function is actually now in the hands of all employees who view and pass on the content to others. The question is how brands can turn that to their advantage, by seeing it as an opportunity to regain some centre ground rather than seeing it as communication anarchy.

Getting to grips with changing media

The collective power of changing media actually presents brand owners with an enormous opportunity to finally use communications to better harmonise people internally and counter any speculation about the brand or its operations. Done well, it can drive a much more positive brand reputation amongst staff: more loyalty, less doubt, more clarity, less misunderstanding. The challenge lies in realising that changing media can help, and then taking a cohesive approach to doing something about it.

And the thing to realise, above all others, is that the root of its potential is that it can engender active conversation, rather than encourage another conversation altogether to take place. The two-way nature of digital media means that conversations which may previously have taken place between individuals or small groups can now be orchestrated, developed and sustained in a way that engages an entire staff.

It's not overstating it to say that the Internet, and the way in which employees can use it to communicate amongst themselves, gives employers an opportunity to whip up and maintain excitement. By communicating the right things in the right ways, organisations can not only improve relations with their internal stakeholders but can also turn their brands into a tangible, cohesive asset amongst their staff, developing employees into not only more loyal (and less sceptical) workers but better advocates for the brand externally.

Sounds great. The question is knowing where to start, and how best to gain a level of cut-through so that the message is well received, perhaps with similar editorial principles applied to those used by conventional media externally, so that content has the desired effect within your four walls. Ideally, it should share the same focus as the brand's external communications, but should be applied and communicated in a different way that's appropriate to how staff feel about the brand, about their work and about their futures. So just like external communication, a thorough and frank understanding of what makes the audiences tick will arm the brand with the best insight in order to ascertain what content will do the job, and how best to get it out there.

In that regard, each and every brand is different, but the knowledge of the audience is crucial to knowing what content to create – its messages, its tone, its balance of information and entertainment, and so on. Beyond that, there are a number of truisms that have, to an extent, always been present in internal communications, but are now bubbling to the fore as social media platforms give fresh impetus to them. According to internal communications consultant and partner at The Team Brand Communications, Cliff Ettridge[1], looking at classic examples of human behaviour in reacting to information dissemination will give brands the cornerstones of communications planning. Ettridge has spent the best part of two decades working in a field that now tends to be labelled 'employee engagement'. In the Internet age, the one that leaps right out is that content will be most compelling, and best understood, when someone adds to it. Ettridge, who has delivered engagement programmes for brands such as BAA, the BBC, the Body Shop, BP, Deutsche Bank, Marks & Spencer, Orange, Royal Mail and Vodafone, puts it simply: scribbling on a sign or wall to deface it where bureaucracy has been badly applied, such as when safety instructions are clearly contrary to common sense, can have enormous communications impact and points to how best to engage employees around a brand.

Such action uses some of the most powerful weapons in the communications arsenal – sarcasm, humour, irreverence – to get the point across. Think of a 'Bill Posters Will Be Prosecuted' notice amended to 'Bill Posters Is Innocent' and you get the picture. The point is that by adding to the original content, far more people will take notice, understand and be inclined to share their perceptions with others. These are daft examples of course, but thinking laterally about how to apply the principle to internal communication makes it clear how, with thorough planning, original content can be orchestrated to entice comment from employees, encourage sharing and take on a life of its own – within a conversation that the brand is part of, and

---

1   Cliff Ettridge http://cliffettridge.wordpress.com

as part of a cohesive communications plan, rather than left to the anarchy of the felt tip pen.

Don't underestimate the fascination

You have a captive audience that cares about the subject matter because it has to – and by applying two-way communication models you can manage brand reputation far more successfully than by issuing doctrines to a nonplussed readership with a sarcastic view on such things. By participating in conversations about the brand and its activities – in a way they want to and about things they care about – employees can understand their employer better, develop stronger belief in the organisation's vision and strategy and, over time, build even greater faith in it.

According to Ettridge, most senior management teams are conscious that employees are generally reluctant to have conversations with them about the things that really matter to the brand or how the organisation is being managed, but the ability to comment and the pulling power of an entire group of people actively wanting to cite their point of view in the open changes the game.

Yet it's still all too easy to get it wrong. 'The people at the top need to learn to get out of the way,' says Ettridge. 'There needs to be a recognition that social media is great for employee engagement precisely because it was created somewhere else, rather than by the people at the top on the inside. There is a sense of ownership over social media content amongst employees, and the brands that will be most successful at managing their reputations internally will be those that latch onto this sense of ownership and tap into its potential rather than trying to replicate, structure or suppress it.'

Therein lies a massive opportunity, and not doing so poses risks too. The risks are that other organisations around you may be doing employee engagement better, and if you don't engage with people in a way that they're rapidly coming to expect in the workplace anyway, then they're left to their own devices. They can form opinions by drawing on content and conversations from the many other sources of influence that now exist out there. If you're not at least engaging them in conversation or, better still, actively participating in all corners of internal discussion about the brand, then you could well be on a sticky wicket, to use a charming English cricketing term that probably needs no further explanation.

Wagging tongues, willing ears

We have mouths, and bits on the sides and fronts of our heads that, if we're lucky, allow us to talk, hear and see. People will always talk, and people will always listen, to some extent. And then they might do something with that information that creates influence, hence the crux of reputation.

You know this, and have known it since childhood. Yet, too often, internal communications planning fails to grasp these most basic tenets. Tongues will always wag and ears will always prick up so that other tongues wag elsewhere. It's called gossip, and most brands see it as a problem rather than something to embrace.

Pre-Internet, internal communication could backfire. Internal memos could become the subject of gossip, and dissent, for all the wrong reasons. Computerised memos often only sped the rate at which gossip spread, rather than turning it to the brand's advantage. The corporate intranet seemed like a great idea when it was heralded as a new way of coalescing staff in the late 1990s. Today's media options call for far broader thinking on how best to communicate information and tap into the human tendency to gossip in digesting and sharing it.

'People don't use structures for this,' says Ettridge. 'When you impose them, people don't want to use them. The Internet is far faster than the tools we've been trying to utilise in years gone by. But it brings with it an increased emphasis on leadership and an increased requirement to share information much faster. Brands need to be actively engaged with their employees all the time, not just saving up choice communiqués for the opportune or seemingly appropriate moment, which typically used to be something issued to staff on a monthly or even less frequent basis.'

People will always be fascinated by what goes on in the boardroom. There will always be a need for certain information to remain confidential, but innovative brands are now experimenting with going far further than they ever have before, using social media to engage employees in conversations and information sharing about what's going on at the top of the organisation, albeit to a restricted extent. Tweeting from, or straight after, board meetings? It's worth thinking about. Listening to employees' conversations online and using them as part of the decision-making process at the top of the company? Seems pretty sensible, depending on the matter in hand. It all adds up to a need for brave and visible leadership, and that's not typically out of synch with the mandates or aspirations of senior managers in many firms. The challenge tends to be in getting them to communicate in ways that still seem alien to many.

The reality is that it is impossible for organisations to prevent their employees from connecting amongst themselves online. Even if access to social media is banned on work equipment, they'll do it at home. If they want to, they'll always find a way. You couldn't gag them before the Internet arrived, and now doing so has the potential to backfire – spectacularly.

Brands today need to have a broad and astute approach to how they consider using any and all forms of media, but also to which tools are the best for certain types of communication. The great corporate intranet experiment may have provided some interesting ways of sharing text-based information, but its stifled and structured nature could not hope to provide a platform for conversations around a brand in the way that social media can. Increasingly, brands are realising that those conversations shouldn't just be in words, but in pictures and moving images too. Just like the conventional media on the outside, they're learning what types of content – governed by editorial nous – are most likely to get people to engage with brands and, ultimately, become a fully signed-up participant in the most important conversations.

There is a reason that subeditors on newspapers lay out pages with pictures first and then flow the words around them: pictures can often communicate things with greater power and precision, can garner greater interest and retention, and so tend to get talked about more. Talk enhances reputation, and the right reputation can lead to sales. Media companies are now learning this about video too, in that it can be a useful instructional tool or can be more engaging that text or static images alone. So brand managers should not just be thinking about how to infiltrate chat online, but how to use a rich tapestry of content to get their people talking, get them thinking about things by the intervention of clued-up content and, as a result, make a positive impact on their brand's reputation.

Being part of the conversations gives brands a direct route to addressing the rumour mill and snuffing out incorrect information. It avoids the risk of dissent or dissatisfaction festering because the company hasn't intervened to address a particular issue. It enables the most important information in the business to be communicated to people in a way that the employees want, and in a way that gives them the ability to be heard.

It needs to be well planned of course. But as Internet-based communication becomes woven into the fabric of our daily lives, smart brands are realising that the risk of not being part of the conversation far outweighs any lingering concerns about the risks of not communicating effectively.

You're a media brand, yes?

It became the flavour-of-the-month a couple of years ago for communications strategists to try to convince all companies that they were now, in the age of Internet-based communication, media companies. That's not to say that they're all publishing companies, but the point is that so many companies and their brands are being talked about online now, and getting involved in those discussions is no longer even optional, so in effect every brand is also a publisher of its own content. It's a fairly largesse way of assessing a pretty obvious situation, but there's something in it.

The reality is that every brand that has any level of public awareness whatsoever has always been, and will always be, a 'media brand' by definition. The difference is in the frequency of attention brands now get from diversifying media, and the expectations of brands to communicate more. As has been covered elsewhere in this book, brands must now find ways to communicate constantly with their audiences, and make the right choices about how and why to do that. From an internal communications standpoint, the implications of being a media brand – a brand that must work media to its advantage – are that it's no longer feasible to write and farm out the odd communiqué here and there or, worse still, be mute.

Changing media has placed a greater demand on brands to communicate internally. Knowing where to start can be tricky though.

Digital media, and the changes that are happening in all other media too, mean that there are more opportunities than ever before for information to be broadcast to staff through a planned programme of communication that is targeted directly at them. The problem is that while digital media may provide a faster way of getting messages across than in a paper- or meeting-based world, it's still just amounts to sticking a message up on a wall and hoping that people will think and say the right sort of things about it, providing of course that they understand it in the first place.

What social media gives – and what owned and earned (or conventional) media can give too if the content is well planned and delivered – is the ability to engage people. In this case, the people who work for the owners of the brand. Engagement is what most social media types will talk about until the cows come home. Engagement is also what many brand managers have been seeking through a series of experimental and, now, more structured and long-term initiatives to capture the eyeballs of the audience and keep them looking. And ideally, the audience will go further than merely looking and will interact with the brand in a way that fosters their loyalty and triggers willingness to both buy and recommend.

Looking inside the organisation, loyalty, commitment to the cause and ambassadorship to the outside world are the typical outcomes that a brand really looks for. But given this, engagement seems to stop short of how a more effective type of internal communication could be applied. Let's face it, the people are already engaged to some extent in that they turn up for work and keep coming back. The ability to go beyond engagement holds new possibilities for brands looking to get more from how they communicate with their own employees. What they should be looking for, although they may not know it, is participation.

Becoming part of the action

Participation with the brand in conversations that affect both the brand and its employees is what organisations should be setting their sights on. It is the only sure-fire way to make employees want to keep conversing with you in order to develop a relationship that moves beyond understanding to trust and, ultimately, to faith.

But you can't make communication work in this way while a 'wall' remains in the middle. First you must engage: to do that you need to have brand content that people can digest, comment on and forward to others. The content has to be relevant, appealing, thought-provoking and in line with the organisation's vision, values and both immediate and long-term priorities. That said, it needs to convey the information with an editorial touch applied, so that it is either really informative or appropriately entertaining. Or both.

Moreover, this content shouldn't just come from the brand itself – it needs to have a human touch. But to attain the kind of attention from the internal audience that turns functional engagement into emotional participation, people have to be not just visible but actually communicating. This is the part that a lot of senior executives seem to either thrive on or struggle with. What should they say, and how often should they say it? Do they actually have to do it themselves, or can it be ghostwritten? How frequent should the communication be and how on earth can the potential level of individual engagement required be fulfilled by any one person? The brand may be aiming for communication that is both authentic and transparent, but what about the things they they're duty bound or commercially compelled to hold back?

These are all valid questions. But there are viable answers to all of them, so long as there is a cohesive internal and external reputation plan in place that is rooted in both the art and science of editorial, joined-up appropriately with other marketing and business development plans and which, most importantly of all, has the full and frank backing of a brand that appreciates that media change equals opportunity as well as threat, and a need to do things differently.

And it's happening anyway

That need, as we've already examined, doesn't just exist because fragmented and digitising media is creating new threats and new opportunities for brands and how they communicate. The truth is that staff are using new media to undertake internal communications themselves, whether you like it or not.

Today, in the UK at least, most statistics show that workers are more likely to be using social media in a personal capacity than not. Conventional media still outshines social media in total audience figures, but that kind of misses the point: the lines between them are blurring anyway, and it is the immediacy and two-way nature of changing media that is forcing communication methods to change, rather than the fact that social media in itself now exists.

As two-way media began to bubble up in the mid-2000s, the people within an organisation became connected to other people within that organisation. Quickly, that mushroomed into lots of people who conversed frequently within the organisation, who perhaps socialised together after work, and who were increasingly connecting to people outside their workplace. The network effect had begun. Without going into the practicalities and possibilities of these interpersonal relationships, let's just draw the simple conclusion that all social media has really done is broken down the differences between how people used to communicate within the brand's four walls and how they did so outside. From an internal communications perspective, looking at the people they work with and who they're connected to online, few people think there's any difference between the content that they share and comment on for work purposes versus personal purposes. It's all just conversation, just like in the real world. Just like in the office kitchen waiting for the kettle to boil, over lunch, or by the proverbial water cooler.

So brands have to realise that content they disseminate to staff with an internal communications agenda will naturally flow outside of the organisation and have prospective influence on external audiences. There is no way of stopping that. And given they're paid employees of the brand, their influence can be potent.

The ability of people to input to media rather than just view or listen to it has extended their level of influence dramatically. It's only replicating or forming an alternative channel to what they were doing already – down the pub, social club, on breaks, or with friends. But given that the facts and opinions people choose to communicate via social media rapidly end up becoming hard-wired into the networks of an external audience, content developed for internal communications has to become more sophisticated, better planned and contain more editorial skill if it is to be commented on favourably beyond the four walls of an organisation.

Learning by listening

Smart planning and editorial skill will only get you on the road though. To really go places with your reputation management internally, you need to go beyond that initial engagement with employees and ensure that they participate fully in conversations about, and with a bearing on, the brand. And the only way you can keep that conversation alive and kicking, and sufficiently fired up to keep reputation developing, is to do what you must do to ensure successful conversation in the real world. Listen.

Someone who talks *at* staff rather than *with* staff will quickly become a bore, or an irritant. Brands must first engage, then drive participation by listening and learning from their communication with personnel. Having an open ear will enable the brand to develop conversation in directions that help fulfil the objectives of the overall communications programme. But being able to learn from what is heard will enable reputation development to be far more successful, as conversations can be kept as relevant as possible, different points of view can be properly considered, new trends can be tackled, and hitherto unheard information can be unearthed. If you play your cards right.

It is practically impossible to anticipate what you might learn from conversations about the brand, or how or when you might learn it. Like many of the most crucial pieces of insight that brands gather in order to plan their communication, some of the most precious information might simply be tripped across at random. The key factor here is actually incredibly complex: it is human behaviour. It might seem the case that human reactions to information can largely be predicted, but in a changing media world, you must remain highly focused on the fickle nature of consumers, the speed at which opinions change and the impact the network effect of social media has on how influence flows. Blink and you might miss the juiciest bits.

By studying human behaviour closely, and acting quickly on fair and accurate interpretations of the data it creates, brands can begin to attain the appropriate balance of command and control in their editorial efforts to manage reputation internally.

It's not just about what they say, or even how they say it – the so-called sentiment with which facts and opinion are expressed online. You also have to learn from the way people engage in order to work out the most effective channels for communicating with them, and from the way they participate to work out the most effective content. It may be that participation in discussion about a certain topic begins, for example, because images of a company event have been posted on a photo-sharing site by an employee. That sparks a humorous debate between employees on Facebook. More employees discuss it offline, fuelling further word-of-mouth appeal. Then later, on Twitter, that brand participates in the now-developed conversation again to bring some new information into view that's relevant, but makes a more serious point about the brand's intentions. At each stage, the ways in which content evolves, how participants react to it and the nuances of how behaviour in a conversation changes between one media and another, all provide vital information in the quest to understand how influence is formed, whether positive or negative. By figuring this out and addressing it in communications planning, greater command over reputation can be gained, even if it can never be controlled.

That planning also needs to consider the expectations that employees will have of the brand when communicating. These, again, may be complex, but certain factors are likely to be constant, just like in real conversation. Initially at least, there is likely to be an expectation that brands may not be completely honest in what they are communicating, or at least will try to polish the information as much as possible. That's an expectation that can be confounded, perhaps immediately or perhaps over a period of time, depending on the brand's communications history and what the brand is.

Typically though, with honesty will come trust, and with trust will come respect; so long as explanation and corroboration are provided in the course of the conversation. It is just not good enough to simply make claims and statements, to communicate fact or instruction, and expect it to stick with internal audiences. Rules, for example, must be explained through participation with the audience as well as just broadcast at them.

According to Ettridge, the tone of the conversation, as well as what is communicated, has a bearing on to what extent the brand is believed and to what extent individual and collective faith enhances its reputation. 'The tone of honesty and the natural expectation of the group of people are what really make a difference to how successful brands are in doing this. They can make belief much more realistic, providing they stick to the truth and are both smart and consistent about how they communicate it. People will form opinions about how honest the brand is going to be based on its past history, their interactions with the people at the top and the way in which each conversation is approached. In the online world, this stuff all comes together, and judgement can be practically instantaneous. It requires a different approach to years gone by, but one that is to a large extent rooted in common sense,' he says.

Innovative companies are not just looking at what they used to do and migrating it to online techniques; they are trying new things too. Measures such as giving an insider's view, where appropriate, on matters being discussed at the top table, and even opening some of the agenda at board meetings to two-way conversations with personnel, are being contemplated. It's all a long, long way from the noticeboard memo but with proper, cohesive planning it has the potential to power reputation gains from the inside, and manage the risks of uncertainty, confusion and lack of faith.

Once the brand has the respect of its employees, participation in conversation can nurture true belief in it. And with belief in the brand, faith in the brand owner – the employer – is within grasp too. It is within the command of the brand's communication.

Summary

- Media change has also changed the way people communicate and respond to information in the workplace. Has this worked more in favour of the employee than the employer?
- Gossip has always happened. Questions will always been asked. There is a natural human curiosity. Brands need to recognise and work with that rather than against it.
- Do these new forms of media change the game for perception of the employer brand by employees?
- Brands should realise that staff have always been influenced by conventional media anyway, but media change has made the points of influence more diverse and given them the ability to engage in conversation. That can be a good thing.
- Employers can use modern media to learning from their staff and listen to them better, for everyone's benefit.

CHAPTER

7

MONITORING AND THE MANAGEMENT OF RISK

Listening to customers and markets has become a crucial function for corporate organisations. #brandanarchy

According to Google's executive chairman, Eric Schmidt, every two days we now create as much information as we did from the dawn of civilisation up until 2003[1]. That's one billion gigabytes. Much of this content is social and includes images, blog posts, comments, tweets and Facebook posts. Conversations about your company and its market are, almost certainly, taking place on the social web right now. Frequently. But how can an organisation possibly make sense of this avalanche of data and figure out what's relevant?

Speaking at a Public Relations Consultants Association (PRCA) event in London about the future of content[2] in June 2011, former director of BBC World Service and Global News, Richard Sambrook, described the period when the audience shifted from having a passive role as the recipient of content from the broadcaster into an active role, where the BBC and its content was actively discussed on the web. 'I distinctly remember the shift because, running BBC News, you were always used to getting one or two letters of complaint per week. Some of them were reasonable, some of them less so, and by and large you would give them a polite reply, noting their point of view,' he says.

---

1 Eric Schmidt data, Techcrunch: techcrunch.com/2010/08/04/schmidt-data/
2 The future of content with a nod to the past, Holmes Report blog post: blog.holmesreport.com/index.php/media/the-future-of-content-with-a-nod-to-the-past/

The medium for complaints changed from letter to email around the end of the 1990s as the Internet moved from a period of intense commercial development into social application. Sambrook, now chief content officer at public relations company, Edelman, describes observing the shift. 'Suddenly, at the turn of the decade, the emails went up and instead of getting one or two we'd get 20 or 30, and then get 200 or 300. Email was treated then like letters; with a polite reply. Then, of course, the weight and the pressure built up as the public really started to express themselves, and some colleagues very rationally started to engage in discussion and emailed back. Then what happened, and this is the key point, is that members of the public started talking to each other *without* us and they would have whole conversations about the BBC and we weren't included. There were whole websites dedicated to discussing what we were doing and we weren't invited. It was extraordinary.'

Your organisation may not be involved in the conversations that are taking place about it but the open nature of the web makes it easier than ever before to monitor what's being written – thanks to Google. Google Alerts provides a real-time alert to content being posted on the web. Used smartly, Google Alerts is an incredibly powerful tool. Every corporate communicator should set up services to alert them, in real time, to email content that is being written about their organisation. Beyond that you can set up alert services in the markets in which you operate.

Twitter, with its 200 million users, is the best service to glean insights on real-time events. Enter your keyword in the search function on the Twitter website and you'll see recent tweets and new ones being posted live. Alternatively, use an application such as Tweetdeck to set up a dedicated search that opens within the application. The search variables within Twitter can be configured to monitor tweets from within a geographic location, from particular named accounts, and hashtags on a given topic. A huge software industry has grown up to deliver insights into corporate communications. More on that shortly, but there's a huge amount that can be achieved at little cost using the techniques that we have described here.

BP: Brutal Predicament

The BP Deepwater Horizon oil spill in the Gulf of Mexico in 2010[3] was one of the biggest corporate disasters in recent times. But it was much more than a public relations crisis; it was a full-blown industrial and environmental disaster and the company faced an onslaught from both conventional and social media. The attacks that the company faced from traditional media, blogs and comments posted on the social web were a very real example of the fact that, as Sambrook described as a factor of his latter years at the BBC, organisations don't own conversations that take place about their brands any more. The damage to BP was well documented in the form of a battered share price and widespread criticism, across all forms of media, from politicians, activists and consumers. BP couldn't start the job of repairing its reputation until it had stopped oil from leaking from the sea bed. The best that it could hope for was to convey its management of the clean-up operation and be utterly transparent in its communication.

'You can't PR away what is essentially a human tragedy. It was a large spill that went on day after day after day. The new dimension in this crisis [that we hadn't seen before] was the fact that it was ongoing, and no one could see the end of it in sight.

---

3 Timeline: BP oil spill, BBC News:
www.bbc.co.uk/news/world-us-canada-10656239

Not only was there was an almost unending flow of oil but also an unending demand for information; and communicators had to work hard to try and meet that demand to give good information,' says Neil Chapman, founder of crisis communications firm, Alpha Voice Communications. He left BP in 2011 after 14 years where his most recent role was in the unified command centre in the United States, set up to respond to the Deepwater Horizon explosion and oil spill in the Gulf of Mexico.

The BP disaster was the first major disaster in which social media played a major role in people calling not only for BP to address the crisis but also in the organisation's response effort. 'Social media played a large part in terms of how people interacted with the company and with the organisations that had useful information to impart. The BP spill demonstrates the challenges there are in trying to monitor what is going on in a crisis because so much of the news coverage, and of the resulting conversations, takes place online, in real time. But real-time conversation gives you an opportunity to get your own message across, which can help to dispel any negative commentary,' adds Chapman.

We had the opportunity to question the former chief executive of BP, Tony Hayward, in June 2011[4] when he spoke at a meeting of the Mandrake networking group in London about the aftermath of the Deepwater Horizon crisis. He said that the conversation frenzy on social media created an immense burden on the communications team on top of the impossible-to-meet demands for information from the conventional media. At the height of the crisis, there were approximately 50 people

---

4   Deepwater Horizon: inside the vicious media war, Speed Communications
    blog post: www.speedcommunications.com/blogs/earl/2011/06/16/
    deepwater-horizon-inside-the-vicious-media-war

from BP working around the clock to counter inaccurate information being posted on social networks such as Facebook and Twitter. It was a social media storm, the like of which had not been seen before. For the team trying to manage it, the pressure was immense and the tide impossible to turn.

Conventional media coverage of the accident and subsequent clean-up operation was 'vicious', says Hayward. This point was mainly levelled at the US media, which led with the story round the clock for weeks. The demand for information from BP was insatiable. Hayward claimed that there were inaccuracies in some of the reporting, and inflated fears about the extent of the spillage and its impact on the Gulf coast. 'We were at war with the media every day. There is no other word for it,' he adds.

Hayward volunteered that despite BP's utmost efforts to communicate clearly, transparently and at breakneck pace, many mistakes were made. Given his time again he says that he would have had more of the senior team around him to handle the media. While the person in overall charge should face the media, the glare can now be so intense that it is too much for one person alone to manage.

Hayward was extremely candid about the lessons he'd learnt from the crisis. The most important was to make sure that expectations are managed when the entire world is watching. This referred to the ongoing efforts to cap the leak on the sea bed. Hayward says that the process and degree of testing required to cap the well weren't adequately communicated, leaving journalists and other commentators to assume that BP had become increasingly desperate to plug the well rather than following a clear process.

More efficient processes, including communications and media planning, may have stopped events spiralling to the extent that they did. A crisis on the scale of Deepwater had never happened before so there was no way of either predicting or mapping out clear plans. BP wasn't sufficiently well prepared but then could any organisation have been adequately prepared for a crisis on this scale? The main lesson for large organisations is that plans for crises such as Deepwater should be made and tested regularly.

Making sense of data

Inevitably, tools are helping brands make sense of the massive amounts of online data, not only in a crisis but in the day-to-day operation of their business. Analytic and monitoring services that would have demanded hefty premiums a decade ago are now available for free. Google Analytics allows a website owner to scrutinise traffic visiting their site. Doubleclick Ad Planner[5] is a media planning tool that provides insights into websites that your target customers are likely to visit. Google Insights for Search allows you to compare search patterns across specific regions, categories, timeframes and web properties. Andrew Smith, managing director of public relations, search marketing and web analytics firm Escherman[6], calls these services Google's 'databases of intentions'.

'Consumers are no longer characterised by demographics; instead they are defined by their search history which is made up of personal motivation and interests. Google almost certainly knows more about your web browsing habits than even your partner and it makes this data freely available via the web. Think of these services as Google's gift to the public relations industry, but it's also a missed opportunity as few practitioners have taken the time or the trouble to understand and use these services. They are broadly the domain of search marketing,' says Smith.

---

5   Doubleclick Ad Planner, Google: www.google.com/adplanner/#siteSearch
6   Escherman: www.escherman.com

Monthly clipping reports of press coverage are in effect dead as a monitoring tool. Companies need real-time data to enable them to respond and adapt their public relations programmes as they are implemented rather than after the event. The feedback loop should be minutes and hours, not weeks or months. Real-time monitoring combined with editorial nous makes this a reality. Richard Bagnall, managing director of Metrica, a global media analysis and public relations measurement firm, cautions against the march of industrialisation in web monitoring. Software analysis is useful in helping to gather data from the web but it requires human intervention to ultimately make sense of the content.

According to Bagnall, results from automated analysis are typically only accurate 50 to 60 per cent of the time. To support his claim he cites a project that analysed and made sense of more than 100,000 pieces of social media content from an 18-month period for a large technology company that had been supplied by one of the leading US social media monitoring companies. Utilising the specialist Boolean search team from sister media planning, monitoring and evaluation company, Durrants, and some technologies developed in-house, Bagnall's team reduced the number of relevant client mentions by a third. Metrica's specialist media analysts then read and evaluated all of the remaining coverage with the result that the data reported back to the client showed that just 33,000 of the posts were actually relevant. One in three.

Man versus machine

In a parallel exercise, Metrica invited some of the leading social media monitoring tool companies to partake in a trial to prove which would be the best partnering company. It challenged them to undertake the same search string over the course of two weeks, and then the Metrica team compared the results.

The volumes returned were widely different, by as much as 50 per cent. Next, Metrica took 1,500 clips from the search results and had media evaluation researchers analyse them for relevance and sentiment, not once or twice, but on three occasions, for positive, negative or neutral sentiment. The results were benchmarked against those from all of the social media measurement companies to really get a sense of which companies were providing the most robust data.

Incredibly, the worst performer was accurate only 29 per cent of the time with its favourability ranking. That's four per cent worse than the one in three wager of leaving the result to pure chance. The next best got the answer right 52 per cent of the time and the best was only 58 per cent accurate. 'If you offer me a lift and there's a 40 per cent chance I won't make it home, I'm not keen to get in in your car. Platform-based monitoring tools alone aren't good enough yet for automated analysis. For the foreseeable future we will need humans to provide context and meaning to the language and the conversation,' says Bagnall.

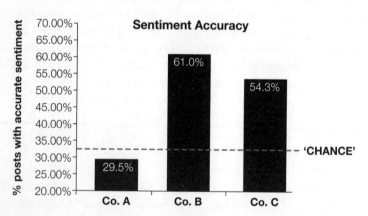

Figure: Percentage of content returned with accurate sentiment analysis during Metrica's analysis of social media monitoring tools (Source: Metrica)

Sentiment analysis and other snake oil

Yet, despite Bagnall's evidence that points to the relative immaturity of monitoring solutions, the market for such tools is saturated and it is nigh on impossible to differentiate one vendor from another. The market for software monitoring tools is overcrowded. A Media Monitoring Solutions Wiki[7] maintained by web marketer and technologist Ken Burbary lists more than 200 so-called solutions. Software firms have spotted the opportunity that the market offers for rapid growth. Scrutinising the context, structure and sentiment of a comment on a blog, tweet or a post on Facebook is complex. It's little wonder that machines struggle.

Consider the following post from a user on Twitter:

'I've just been to Waitrose. Great value but parking with kids is awful. Thinking of trying M&S but it's a longer drive.'

The sentiment for Waitrose is both positive and negative. The shopper likes Waitrose because it offers good value for money but finds it difficult to park at the store that they visited. Automated sentiment analysis would almost certainly score the post as neutral. But in fact, a human being would recognise the sentiment of the post as negative for Waitrose as it is about to lose a customer to M&S. Likewise, the post is both positive and negative for M&S and would most likely be marked up as neutral by an automated monitoring tool. M&S is gaining a new customer but its store is further away than Waitrose. A human would mark the sentiment of the post as positive for M&S.

7 A Wiki of Social Media Monitoring Solutions, Ken Burbary: http://wiki.kenburbary.com/

Only a human being would be guaranteed to recognise the post as negative for Waitrose and would have the insight to flag the customer to be contacted by Waitrose to determine if their parking experience could be improved. Likewise, a human being working for another supermarket or online grocer would recognise the potential to attract a new customer by persuading them to try *their* store or shop online.

For now, language beyond simple assertions of like or dislike and love or hate is too complex for machines to grasp. Moreover, a simple red, amber or green traffic light commonly used by sentiment monitoring tools doesn't convey the complexity or meaning of the message. During an hour-long period in December 2010, we counted 45 messages on Twitter relating to M&S and more than 90 for Waitrose. It is going to take considerable resources and organisational change for companies to be able to process and respond appropriately to such a high volume of customer contact. There is a reason that some organisations, notably the majority of retail banks, don't entertain engaging on social networks such as Twitter. They know they wouldn't be able to cope with the sheer volume of conversation. These organisations are actively blocking social interaction channels because they know they will be inundated with criticism and complaints.

Measure outcomes not outputs

Measuring the success of a communications campaign is not trivial. For now, the industry is measuring outputs. This is a fundamental error according to Bagnall, who believes that the public relations industry is in danger of being bombed back into the dark ages in which we used proxies such as advertising equivalent value (AVE) and column inches as a means of determining the success of a campaign. AVEs were created as a means of benchmarking the results from a public relations campaign. The cost of buying the physical space in a media outlet was calculated and multiplied by a factor of three or four in recognition of the fact that editorial has more value as a means of influence than an advertisement. Spot the flaw. The implicit goal of any campaign was to prove that the total AVE value was two or three times the cost of buying the space, thus claiming a respectable return on investment. The industry has come a long way but remains wedded to counting outputs as a metric of success. Blog posts, Facebook 'likes', comments and tweets (like headline fonts, photograph sizes and circulation figures) are all logged and charted as a demonstration of success. 'We're still counting and looking at quantity but it's meaningless without context. You can't have a one size fits all approach without disregard for the business', says Bagnall.

Herein is the issue. The public relations industry has avoided creating a universal measurement system because it deemed it too difficult. No two public relations campaigns are the same. It's an issue that has challenged practitioners for the last 50 years and, as a result, led to the public relations industry being sidelined because, unlike other business functions, it is unable to show a relationship between investment and return. As a result, the industry has grasped onto false metrics of advertising value equivalent (AVE), and the opportunities created by a campaign for interaction with the target audience, in an attempt to prove its worth. Fixing this problem requires industry-wide education and it needs everyone operating within the industry to challenge the objectives set for a public relations campaign and ensure that they are aligned directly to the objectives of the business. The measurement framework, or infrastructure, then needs to be created to support the measurement of the outcomes of the public relations campaign and demonstrate return on investment. It is not going to be easy, but it's a difficult issue that lies at the root of reputation of the public relations industry itself. We'll look at how some individuals and organisations within the industry are tackling this issue head on in Chapter 8.

Flawed metrics: reach and readership

In a bid to demonstrate the pointlessness of counting variables such as reach and readership, Realwire's Adam Parker and Escherman's Andrew Smith teamed up in August 2010[8] to undertake a project that demonstrated the difference between the editorial reach of a website versus the engagement of Internet users that visited the site.

'For decades, public relations has been viewed as a means to gain editorial coverage that provided the greatest number of opportunities to see a mention of a company name, at a significantly lower cost than advertising. Because the means of providing a verifiable link between editorial coverage and business impact was either prohibitively expensive or just not possible, there has been a largely accepted assumption that positive press coverage is valuable. The notion of measuring engagement with editorial content was largely theoretical. Circulation and readership figures were treated as proxies for engagement,' says Smith.

If a publication had 10 million online readers, then the assumption is that a large proportion must, in some way, be engaged with some or all of the content. Yet how can we be sure which content and to what degree? But for online PR, Google tools provide hard numbers. Parker and Smith define reach as the number of views that a page receives, and engagement as the amount of time that a person spends on a page. The pair

---

8 Online news title readership and engagement analysis Slideshare presentation, Andrew Smith and Adam Parker: www.slideshare.net/ realwire/online-news-titles-readership-and-engagement-analysis-280710

scrutinised the reach versus engagement for 50 online news sites ranging from *The Guardian* to *The Economist* and found that visitors spend a widely varying amount of time on different news sites; the pair also predicted how many words visitors are likely to have read per page. They found that, for the period of the study, the average UK visitor to *The Economist* website spends around 122 seconds per page whereas the average UK visitor to the *Vogue* site spends around 33 seconds per page. If you accept that a typical reader can consume around 200 words of content per minute then a visitor to *The Economist* is going to consume around 400 words versus around 100 for a *Vogue* reader.

As a general rule, specialist titles seem to have lower numbers of visitors and page views, but tend to have far higher engagement with content. For consumer titles and newspaper website, the opposite is the case. There is one exception to the rule. News sites such as Reuters act as a syndication service and have both a high level of reach and engagement. A UK visitor to the Reuters website spends 214 seconds per website consuming more than 700 words. The lessons for online public relations are clear: plan your campaigns and target content at sites in which your audience is engaged; and there is little value to be gained in chasing sites with large circulation numbers as engagement is likely to be low. Finally, and this maxim has always been the case, the higher up a story the mention of your organisation, the greater prominence it achieves and the more likely it is to be read. Some things never change then.

Peer metrics

A group of social media analytics firms are now specialising in tracking and ranking the contributions of individuals within social networks. These include Klout, based in San Francisco, and PeerIndex, based in London. Klout measures a user's influence across the social web by collecting data from each of the major social networks. Scores range from one to 100, with higher scores representing a wider and stronger sphere of influence based on reach, amplification and network size.

PeerIndex takes this approach a stage further by scrutinising activity, audience and authority. It also provides a single score for a user's social media influence but, perhaps most usefully, it breaks down scores across a range of topic areas which include arts, technology, science, medicine, lifestyle, sports, politics and business. This recognises that, while a user might be influential about technology, they may not be about food or football.

Peer metrics are a shortcut to evaluating an individual's relative influence on a topic within a social network. They provide a mechanism by which to identify the influence of one individual versus another on a given topic. This, in particular, is the benefit of PeerIndex over Klout. Its application in developing and planning marketing campaigns are clear. PeerIndex allows me to identify the thought leaders in a given market and reach out to them via their social network. Peer metrics will almost certainly become part of the due diligence process for human resource teams and it is inevitable that organisations will start to use peer metrics as a means to prioritise responses to complaints made via social media. Customer service teams that receive large volumes of social media traffic will inevitably prioritise an individual with a higher peer metric.

Can crowds really be wise?
Much of the information created on the web, especially the social web, is utter nonsense. It's a common viewpoint for which you'd struggle to put up a case for the defence on a Sunday morning on Twitter. We've already explored in

Chapter 2 how social networks don't check facts. Anyone can publish and share information, irrespective of motivation. That openness is a benefit as well as a challenge. It means organisations can face assault from anyone armed with an Internet connection. In this section we'll look at what brands can do to verify the authenticity of content and what are the legal jurisdictions on the web.

In *The Wisdom of Crowds*, James Surowiecki[9] described how information is shared and assimilated by a group resulting in decisions that are better for the group than those that would be made by any single individual. We've already cited numerous examples of organisations being called out via social media for failing to meet the expectation of their audience. Technology both facilitates and accelerates communication by crowds. But can crowds make the wrong call? Almost certainly, the answer is yes.

August 2011 saw riots on the streets of several British cities, triggered by the death of Mark Duggan at Tottenham Hale in north-east London, apparently at the hands of a police firearm specialist. Messages spread quickly on social networks wherever trouble occurred. But for every tweet or Facebook post which reported areas to avoid, there were numerous which cited rumour or speculation.

In this instance, the crowd panicked. At one point during the crisis, an image circulated on Twitter of the army assembling tanks at Bank underground station. It was sufficiently credible to be reposted and retweeted, and so spread quickly from mobile device to mobile device. Anyone who had opened the image on a device with a larger screen would have seen the

---

9 Surowiecki, James. *The Wisdom of Crowds*. Anchor Books, reprint edition, 16 Aug 2005.

Arabic writing on the side of the tanks. A Google search turned up the original source as being Tahrir Square, Cairo. The image had been taken earlier in the year, in February 2011, when the Egyptian military there cracked down on protestors.

Crap detection: verifying Internet sources

News organisations such as the Associated Press, the BBC and Thomson Reuters are working hard to verify content sourced from social networks as part of their news-gathering efforts so that original content can be used as a source. In locations such as Syria, where governments outlaw media organisations, social media provides a useful context to the news-gathering process but only when content has been verified. News organisations can invest significant effort in qualifying a source but what of the individual that spots an insightful message in their newsfeed? How should you verify it before sharing it with your network or retweeting the content? Organisations need to be able to determine the authenticity of an individual and the content that they share in social networks. It has implications for sharing and responding to comments.

Howard Rheingold, author of *Smart Mobs: The Next Social Revolution*[10], published in 2003, believes that social media literacy is critical for anyone using the Internet. Rheingold is a critic, writer, and teacher; his specialties are based on the cultural, social and political implications of modern communication media. He cites five competences that he believes are critical for any Internet user, namely attention, participation, cooperation, network awareness and critical

---

10 Rheingold, Howard. *Smart Mobs: The Next Social Revolution*. Perseus Books, 2003.

consumption. It is this latter attribute, namely critical thinking, or what Rheingold calls 'crap detection'[11], that we should all have when searching and assigning credibility to content that we consume online and detect information tainted by ignorance, misinformation or deception.

Rheingold credits Ernest Hemingway with originally inventing the phrase 'crap detection' in an interview for the US magazine *Atlantic* in 1954. Hemingway is reported to have said, 'Every man should have a built-in automatic crap detector operating inside him. It also should have a manual drill and a crank handle in case the machine breaks down.'

Detecting the credibility of content online starts by asking: who is the author? 'If you can't find one, or if the source is hidden behind a pseudonym, turn the scepticism meter to the top of the dial,' says Rheingold. Web domain websites such as easywhois.com enable the registrar of a domain to be checked. If the source provides a means to ask questions, communicate or comment, it improves the chance that the content will be authentic. The same rules apply in social media. Is the original source a real person with a photo, contact information and credible biography, or is it clearly a spammer? Secondly, scrutinise the context. Does the author have prior citations on the Internet? Do they link to reputable sources? Do people link to their content? Who do they engage with online? And what sort of conversations are they having? Thirdly, use social media analytics tools such as Klout and PeerIndex, combined with search engines, to interrogate the social media 'capital' of an individual.

11 Rheingold, Howard. 'Crap Detection 101', *San Francisco Chronicle*, 30 June 2009.

During a breaking news story such as the 2011 London riots, time is compressed and it becomes more difficult to perform these checks, but that is arguable that they are more critical than ever. Individuals have a responsibility to their networks to authenticate the credibility of content before sharing it with their networks. Do not ever rely on spoon-fed information from the Internet. Everyone needs to be their own information analyst and be able to question the authenticity of content. Facts can be checked using your network but it also means venturing beyond the echo chamber of your immediate community to be exposed to alternative viewpoints.

Legal process on the Internet

What happens when its goes badly wrong? Social media is a brave new world of free speech according to its proponents. It's an indeterminate location online that is open, borderless and free from the shackles of editorial control where activists are able to communicate freely. But what happens when the conventions of a social network don't provide an adequate mechanism for response or retribution? Individuals and organisations need a mechanism to protect their reputation and for now that's still the law. Conventional wisdom says that it is not possible for media law to hold up online and cite the *Trafigura* case in October 2009. Trafigura (a large international oil, metals and minerals trader) obtained an injunction to prevent an MP from tabling a question about the company in Parliament. Media commentators got very excited when a huge number of conversations on Twitter seemingly forced Trafigura's lawyers, Carter-Ruck, to back down. But, contrary to popular opinion, the injunction was overturned following an appeal by lawyers from *The Guardian* and not the debate on Twitter.

Did we observe a game-changing moment? Not a chance. There are currently more than 300 so-called superinjunctions holding tight in the UK. Is the Trafigura incident a one off? It almost certainly is not. But don't let the Trafigura case fool you. While we would always advocate a legal response as the last resort, social media is not beyond the reach of copyright, defamation or privacy laws, according to media litigator Gideon Benaim, partner at Schillings.

'The law of defamation applies equally online as well as offline, whatever the legal jurisdiction. A story used to break without warning and then die away relatively quickly. Now, thanks to social media, stories frequently bubble under for a time and, if they can be dealt with before the tipping point, a crisis can often be averted. When a story does break, social media typically extends its lifecycle far beyond traditional means. It is important that corporate organisations have a plan for dealing with attacks on their reputation,' he says.

The judiciary's attitude to media in the UK has been to treat it as they would any other form of social media and apply the same laws of copyright and defamation. It's booming business for lawyers who are active in this area as cases come before the courts on a weekly basis. Here's an example. Jeremiah Barber, who posted child pornography along with a defamatory comment on the Facebook page of his former friend Raymond Bryce, was fined £10,000 in July 2010[12]. Barber, who had fallen out with Bryce over an £80 debt, removed the post within 24 hours. But Bryce contended that there had been 11 links to the post, two comments from viewers, and more than 800 people would have been able to view the material and so he sued Barber for the stress he endured.

---

12 Law student wins £10,000 after being branded a paedophile: www. telegraph.co.uk/technology/facebook/7912731/Law-student-wins-10000-after-being-branded-a-paedophile-on-Facebook.html

Protecting identity in networks

Social networks deal quickly with trademark infringements and cases of deliberate misinformation. Trademarks provide legal protection against a brand name being hijacked online and contrary to perceived wisdom, the process of enforcement is straightforward. Both advertising and social networks recognise the importance of protecting a brand online and, once alerted to abuse, will typically move quickly to correct the situation. Trademark owners should follow guidance set out by individual network owners.

Brand protection

International design and innovation company, Seymourpowell[13], had to enforce trademarks on Facebook, Twitter and Google's advertising network. When Seymourpowell came to register its company name on Twitter, it found that someone had got there first. But by following Twitter's trademark violation process, the company was able to claim @seymourpowell for itself. 'The process was very simple. We completed a violation claim and within a matter of days Twitter released the account to us. Similarly, Facebook removed a spurious page that was hijacking our company name in a matter of hours,' says Tim Duncan, Seymourpowell's head of public relations.

Seymourpowell has also used its trademark to successfully stop competitors from bidding on its name as a Google AdWord. Google respects trademarks and prohibits infringements by advertisers. 'In each instance of abuse we followed Google's advice and contacted the site owner that was abusing our company name as a paid-for search term, pointing out that it was a trademark. In each instance they ceased their activity immediately,' says Duncan. Organisations must monitor and police their trademarks online and take immediate action to address breaches. A robust monitoring policy is critical.

Whether or not a business wants to invest in online and social media monitoring depends entirely on whether it wants to listen to the conversations taking place online about its business and the markets in which it operates. We're often asked to explain the return on investment of social media. I encourage anyone who asks that question to head online and explore the conversations taking place around their business and its markets and determine whether they have a value to their organisation. We suggest that they almost certainly will.

Summary
- Conversations are taking place online about your organisation and its markets. Social media monitoring enables you to listen to what is being said.
- Monthly clipping reports are useless as a monitoring tool. Software tools enable online content to be monitored and recorded in real time.
- Automated sentiment monitoring should be complemented with human analysis.
- Plan campaigns where your audience is engaged, not by chasing large and almost certainly irrelevant audiences.
- Peer metrics are a shortcut to evaluating an individual's relative influence on a topic within a social network.

- Editorial intelligence is required to determine the credibility of a source online.
- Legal process is the final recourse for defamation and intellectual property infringements online.

CHAPTER

8

MEASURING REPUTATION

From an obsession with counting stuff to an obsession with measuring the right stuff. But what next? #brandanarchy

Reputation is the result of what you do, what you say and what people therefore think and say about you.

So the digitisation of media – all media – can actually help in the measurement of reputation, because what you do and say, and what people therefore say or 'hear' about you, can be tracked. It can be assessed and analysed. It can become the subject of a multitude of impressive graphs.

And if you engage in the right way, or ask the right questions, it can also enable you to find out what the audience truly thinks about your brand, which can have an underlying, yet powerful influence on your brand's reputation.

Yet while the management of reputation is the classic definition of PR, many marketers are now looking for faster gains from both social and conventional media campaigns. The drive to assess business outcomes – the direct commercial gains that a brand makes by undertaking an external public relations exercise – is rapidly gaining ground as media digitisation, a joined-up desire to be able to measure those outcomes and better analysis tools for doing so combine to take the measurement of public relations, traditionally largely a random activity, to new heights.

Conversely, if brands are able to measure the success of public relations exercises by clinically assessing business outcomes, so they should also be able to assess the negative impact that adverse circumstances have on commercial fortunes. While this is an area that, to date, has been far less explored than its more positive outcome cousin – public relations tends to like to focus on the good stuff; it is in its nature – it could have equally powerful value for brands wanting to quantify and best manage their exposure to risk in an increasingly digitised and now two-way media world.

The sum of this, however, is that digitisation brings with it the ability to measure things better, and that is forcing the industry to do so in a way that puts a monetary value on the outcomes of investment. To date, most of the work has been in measuring the short-term impact, or the effect, of one-off campaigns. Over time, measurement will have to broaden its horizons to address the impact of perception and, therefore, reputation.

The important thing, ultimately, is that the correlation between public relations investment and measurable change in reputation becomes an identifiable and understandable item in the profit and loss accounts of brands. We are not there yet. But we are edging closer, and the digitisation of media means that – without the application of supposed 'industry science' – that correlation is not far from reality.

Equally, though, as with all other types of sales and marketing activity, being able to count to the penny what impact an activity has had on the bottom line is a fool's errand. This is because the time and, therefore, cost of doing so may outweigh the benefits, and because we are ultimately talking about the hearts and minds of human beings, and so any measurement can never be absolute.

Making it count

The modern public relations industry has an obsession with counting things.

But actually, public relations has always been preoccupied with counting – it's just that a lot of that counting, at least from an evaluation perspective, has historically been of limited value. In some cases, it has been next to meaningless, and in most cases the counting has been served up with a hefty dollop of claims about how the results prove that the editorial coverage gained makes a marked difference to the business. Largely, such claims were wholly unsubstantiated.

Today, public relations is able to get much closer to a meaningful answer to the eternal question: 'Is all this public relations stuff really worth it for my business?' We don't yet have the full answer, but it is being put together, piece by piece. What evaluation experts in the industry are still doing is counting things – only now, because of media digitisation, they're able to do so with greater accuracy and with a greater sense of meaning. And it's largely automated.

Counting alone will not get you very far, though. Imagine you have swathe of positive reviews of a new product on Internet news sites, but one scathing one in a national Sunday newspaper, and sales have been thin since launch. Do those positive reviews have any real commercial value in this case, regardless of how many you achieved? Yet if every piece of editorial had been positive, what notional value would you place on the newspaper piece versus that of the others?

So, volume alone is something of an evaluation cul-de-sac. The quality of editorial – what it says – matters too, but so does whether the 'right' people read it, how and where they read it, the extent to which they are influenced by it and, ultimately, whether it compels them to buy from you immediately or more open to buying from you in the future. Moreover, there's the question of whether they will recommend you to others, which has long been held up as one of the most powerful factors of editorial influence yet continues to be one of the trickier ones to evaluate in raw commercial terms.

Data with destiny

What can brand managers count meaningfully today then, given the upheaval in the media and the fact that there are both direct and indirect routes to influencing audiences through editorial? Well, the straight answer is that they can count pretty much anything: readership, page impressions, resulting search rankings, you name it – if the data is available from the media in question, totting up is a relatively simple exercise. The number of inbound sales enquiries can even be measured and attributed either directly or indirectly to the investment, providing the relevant product or service is purely being publicised through editorial.

The problem is that this only tells you whether the volume of your publicity is increasing, not whether that makes any difference to your business. An obvious and much-made statement, perhaps, but it remains the case. Analytical tools are springing up practically every day to help brands attach some commercial logic to the content that appears about them, or their markets, on the Internet. These aim to measure things like the degree of influence exerted by editorial over a set period of time, the sentiment of the audience towards a brand, how social media conversations about a particular brand compare with those about other brands, and the impact of social media content on editorial content in conventional media. This is all extremely useful information, and a lot of people have invested bags of energy, time and money in enabling its accessibility. What it doesn't tell us, of course, is whether people have opened, or will open, their wallets as a direct consequence of having viewed or been told about the editorial. A consumer might have long harboured strong feelings about the Ferrari brand, read a lot about it and will always circulate the brand's content to other interested parties when it's spotted. But unless he wins the pools, he won't be buying one anytime soon.

The summary is this – brands now have ready access to far more data than they've ever had before in order to try to assess the value of 'their' editorial. Yet this value largely remains a likely or best-guess value, as putting pound signs in front of the results of public relations investment is the only way that public relations can ever be charted all the way through to true commercial outcomes.

It means that there is still much to do to make public relations measurable to the enduring satisfaction of finance managers and, therefore, to all stakeholders. Yet if your brand is being slated by a braying mob of consumers across the world which ends up eroding years of careful imaging-building, you don't really care about how much commercial impact the editorial and its influence are having. You just want it to stop, because the commercial outcome is pretty bloody obvious.

Does it really do that?

But even if we were able to show in pounds and pence how successful a public relations campaign has been, was it really the editorial in question that forced the purchase? Would the customer have bought the product or service anyway? Was a customer about to buy it but then circumstances changed and, for some unknown reason, they decided not to?

PR is not alone in facing this challenge over absolute proof.

Here's an example. Imagine that a salesman's new tie (which he bought with his own money, from a reputable store, in a sale) may have had some impact on a customer being sufficiently impressed to sign a £10 million contract with the salesman's organisation. Where is the saving on the cost of the tie, or the salesman's salary, pro rata to the amount of time invested in winning the contract, in the P&L? But the point is that, rather than wanting to undertake extremely granular measurement so that every element of public relations investment can be commercially assessed, brands should instead focus on the bigger picture, and then drill down to specifics – where that makes logical sense.

There is a level of detail that is, ultimately, counterproductive. Yet what the digitisation of media – conventional *and* social – gives brands is a unilateral power to at least see what it is they're dealing with when it comes to influence over reputation. To the letter. Their challenge is to make sense of what they see, and apply commercial value to it in a way that's appropriate for them.

There are limits to what can be done. You may be able to see everything that's going on that could conceivably affect brand reputation, and have the right tools and the right approach to make sense of it. You may be able to apply that data to your commercial goals so that the impact on your success can be assessed pragmatically and logically. You may be able to draw a thick, straight line between what you spend on public relations and what money it makes for you.

But beyond that, brands must realise that regardless of how technologically advanced media and routes to editorial become, PR's value will never be measured through purely clinical means. That's because we are dealing with human beings, and human beings are fickle. The only way you can ever truly assess the commercial impact of editorial influence over a customer is to go and ask them whether the editorial was the sole reason for their purchasing decision.

And even then they may not remember, or may not want to admit that they've been swayed.

The search goes on

There is a proverbial elephant in the proverbial room though. Search.

The impact of editorial on your reputation is no longer just that lots of people may see it on one particular day if they read the newspaper, tune in to the TV or listen to the radio. Impact is lasting, because much of the editorial content is preserved for eternity on the Internet, and is also voluntarily sought out by audiences. Rather than browsing media and chancing across content, they actively seek it and search engines retrieve it for them.

Moreover, the further up a search list that some editorial content appears, the greater the inference that it has more influence, and so the more likely it is to affect brand reputation. This is clearly an area where conventional and digital media are coming together to create a combined impact on reputation but, more importantly, there are profound implications for reputation when audiences actively go looking for editorial about brands – or set up trackers to automate the process – rather than effectively waiting for it to fall into their laps.

Does that really matter? Won't audiences probably, or eventually, see the content anyway, so all search does is drag it to their attention earlier? Those points are true, but pretty primitive in the scheme of things. Search is becoming a major force in purchasing decisions for all manner of goods and services. What is written or 'said' about your brand can have a direct impact on decisions to buy, while archived editorial content can impinge on brand reputation for years to come, depending on the publisher, the search terms and the circumstances.

The positive thing about search for public relations practitioners is that it can be extremely straightforward to measure some commercial outcomes. Take, for instance, someone searching for a product, finding that a national newspaper's online review of it is third in a Google search under the product brand name, reading the review and then clicking on the brand's website to purchase. The audit trail that this leaves is like the consumer's thought process mapped out for all to see – the downside is that negative editorial will be just as prominent, if not more so, and it can linger in archives indefinitely.

There are myriad implications for brand reputation that stem from the mechanics of search and how it is used to track down editorial content. What's more, those mechanics are constantly changing, so there is rule book that can be adopted now and will stand the rest of time for brand managers worried about the potency and longevity of good and bad news. The precise impact that search results have on reputation is very much a work in progress, although for the time being it is an inflammatory concern for brands already struggling to deal with how technology has made the world of media a far more dangerous territory.

Search is another facet of modernising media that the public relations industry must wrestle with as it works to find its feet in a very different landscape.

What is the public relations industry doing?

Before social media became mainstream, most public relations industry conversations about evaluation tended to go in circles. They were small circles and, normally, the same circles. Progress it was not. The ability for audiences to answer back and engage in direct dialogue with brands has forced the issue – public relations is now having to develop a commercially mature and resilient approach to evaluation for the first time. In fairness, media modernisation was driving that change anyway, but the advent of social media put the need for a new kind of evaluation beyond question.

For a while, the question was where to start. Then the industry, led by those with most to gain from a more progressive approach, began to make noises that PRs would have to agree on a basic set of principles for measuring returns on investment in order that we could then work collectively to establish how best to do it.

What the public relations industry needs to do, and is working hard to do, is to get brands to understand what they're up against, and what choices they need to make in determining an evaluation model that is right for their business. That alone is not easy, but to compound matters it's a moving target – further media change will only make evaluation even more complex, while further digitisation will give us more things to measure.

The public relations industry is inching towards the type of evaluation that modern media will require. Meanwhile, calls from businesses for public relations measurement to be absolute continue unabated; businesses want clinical measurement of public relations investment.

Death of Advertising Value Equivalent (AVE)

AVE was finally effectively 'buried' as a means of evaluation in June 2010 by the Association for Measurement and Evaluation of Communication (AMEC) which brought together a group of experts in Barcelona to agree on a set of measurement and evaluation principles. The Barcelona Principles were conceived by Barry Leggetter, executive director of AMEC, after what he describes as a 'light bulb moment' to tackle one of the key issues that the public relations industry had always avoided; the development of a universal framework for the measurement of PR.

Leggetter acknowledges the drive of Dr David B. Rockland, partner and CEO of Ketchum Pleon Change and Global Research and chairman of AMEC's North American Chapter in taking the Barcelona Principles idea forward – and making it work. The resulting Barcelona Principles[1] consist of seven statements that

---

1 The Barcelona Principles, AMEC: www.amecorg.com/amec/Barcelona%20 Principles%20for%20PR%20Measurement.pdf

aim to move the public relations profession from measuring outputs towards evaluating outcomes:

1. Goal setting and measurement are important
2. Media measurement requires quantity and quality
3. AVEs are not the value of public relations
4. Social media can, and should be, measured
5. Measuring outcomes is preferred to measuring media results (outputs)
6. Organisational results and outcomes should be measured whenever possible
7. Transparency and replicability are paramount to sound measurement

'We're proud of the fact that Barcelona put measurement firmly on the agenda for the first time. It defined a measurement framework and it has been rewarding to see how the industry has taken the Principles to heart. Each week we see announcements from public relations agencies and organisations announcing that they are ditching AVEs. It has resulted in initiatives by public relations organisations worldwide,' says Leggetter. In the UK, the Chartered Institute of Public Relations (CIPR) and the Public Relations Consultants Association (PRCA) have both established measurement toolkits which incorporate the Barcelona Principles. An AMEC taskforce subsequently developed a measurement framework called Valid Metrics that identifies possible metrics for individual public relations programmes[2].

---

2 Valid Metrics for PR Measurement, AMEC: http://ameceuropeansummit. org/amecorgdocs/ValidMetricsFramework7June2011PrintVersion.pdf

AMEC has set a long-term vision and recognises that is going to take a generation to establish an industry-wide measurement framework. It is making a genuine bid to tackle measurement and develop a worldwide standard by bringing together the Public Relations Society of America (PRSA), the International Communications Consultancy Organisation (ICCO), the CIPR, the PRCA and the Council of PR Firms. But it is also engaging directly with public relations agencies and organisations to develop a robust measurement framework. It is by adopting such an internationally consultative approach through such initiatives that AMEC will establish the Barcelona Principles as standard operating procedure in the public relations industry. AMEC's Measurement Agenda 2020 priorities are:

1. How to measure the return on investment (ROI) of public relations
2. Create and adopt global standards for social media measurement
3. Measurement of public relations campaigns and programmes needs to become an intrinsic part of the public relations toolkit
4. Institute a client education programme such that clients insist on measurement of outputs, outcomes and business results, from public relations programmes

The business of influence

The pursuit of a robust measurement system for the public relations industry is something that Philip Sheldrake seeks to tackle in *The Business of Influence*[3]. 'Anybody who tells you that public relations cannot be measured just hasn't investigated it

---

3 Sheldrake, Philip. *The Business of Influence*. Wiley, 2011.

in a professional manner as they should do for their employer's sake or their clients' sake, and for their own professional sake,' says Sheldrake.

Influencer relations is a buzz phrase of recent times. 'It's been hijacked to mean different things. If you look at the dictionary definition, what it effectively means is that we've been influenced when we think in a way we wouldn't otherwise have thought or when we do something we wouldn't otherwise have done,' says Sheldrake. Sheldrake is making a bid to help the public relations industry grow up and adopt management discipline. There has traditionally been a disconnect between public relations and other parts of an organisation which results from the industry's inability to prove return on investment or be measurably accountable in the way that other marketing disciplines do. This issue lies at the core of the reputation of the industry and it being recognised as a strategic, rather than a tactical, tool.

Sheldrake's solution has been to investigate the Balanced Scorecard, a strategic performance management tool devised by Professor Robert Kaplan and Dr David Norton in the 1990s, and augment it for marketing and public relations. The Balanced Scorecard is a structured methodology that is used by managers to keep track of business activities within their remit. According to the Balance Scorecard Institute[4]:

'The Balanced Scorecard has evolved from its early use as a simple performance measurement framework to a full strategic planning and management system. The [...]

---

4 Balanced Scorecard Basics, Balanced Scorecard Institute: www.balancedscorecard.org/BSCResources/AbouttheBalancedScorecard/tabid/55/Default.aspx

balanced scorecard transforms an organisation's strategic plan from an attractive but passive document into the "marching orders" for the organisation on a daily basis. The framework [...] not only provides performance measurements, but helps planners identify what should be done and measured. It enables executives to truly execute their strategies.'

Sheldrake's Influence Scorecard is a subset of the Balanced Scorecard, containing all the key performance indicators (KPIs) stripped of the typical siloed departmental thinking that permeates the influence disciplines such as marketing, public relations, internal communications, public affairs, and customer service. The latter point is important as it removes the tension between functional roles and focuses on outcomes. The scorecard is both a philosophy of setting strategy against the six influence flows around an organisation and a set of checks and balances that demand the setting, scrutiny and reporting of progress against defined targets.

Most importantly, the Influence Scorecard approach recognises the multifaceted, multidisciplinary and complex way in which influence goes-around-comes-around. While the structure, culture and processes of the typical organisation are rooted in traditional media, technologies and understanding of business strategy definition and execution, the Influence Scorecard helps organisations adapt to 21st-century media and disintermediation, the latest Internet, web and mobile technologies, and the best-practice thinking for business strategy and execution.

The key point is that there are no easy answers or one solution such as AVE that fits all. Sheldrake summarises the issue neatly. 'If your market is unique and your vision is unique, then by definition your strategy is unique; therefore, your execution is unique and your measurement and evaluation will be unique. But you're beholden to actually make sure you invest in the resources to monitor progress otherwise you don't know what you're doing from one week to the next and you don't know whether it's working or not,' he says.

At the AMEC Lisbon conference in 2011, delegates decided that AMEC's number one priority should be the development of an approach to distilling the return on investment of public relations type activities. 'Anyone with a general understanding of associated influence disciplines – from branding to advertising, HR to supplier management, retail to packaging – will recognise this challenge. And yet all such investments are intangible, and intangible assets only have value when they're "in the mix". It's complex, yet executives hanker for the simple. I hope the Influence Scorecard increasingly helps executives appreciate the complexity and ensures that the potential to influence and be influenced is exploited cohesively throughout the organisation, with ROI built in. Ultimately, the ease and effectiveness with which we manage and learn from influence flows is integral to the ways all stakeholders interact with organisations to broker mutually valuable, beneficial relationships,' says Sheldrake.

If not reputation, what about influence?

So you now know how you can keep score better. But how do you know what actions scored the most points? How do you know what your priorities are in trying to milk those potentially glacial influence flows?

First you need to be able to segment your audience, which in itself is complicated. Then you need to establish, within those brackets and overall, which people have the greatest influence. On sales, on brand perception, on brand awareness, on legislation, on whatever will assist your brand, fairly and legally, with its objectives. But most important of all for sustained success you must establish which people have the greatest influence on your brand's reputation.

The Internet has helped to automate, and even identify, a good deal of that. You need to interpret the data wisely, but it's perfectly feasible to observe and work out which people have the greatest influence on your brand, how they're connected, the extent to which others listen to and have faith in them, and how influence might build amongst those people. That's where the multitude of social media monitoring tools come in, but there are data feeds to consider from other media too: what's being said in conventional media and how is that impacting upon conversations in all forms of Internet-based media? What type of engagement are you having with the audience on your own media? Are those the same people, or different?

But data will only get you so far – it's what you make of it and how you choose to apply meaning to it that counts. Brands need to look past what is said about them online; instead they need to find out who those doing the talking or conversation-broking are connected to. You need to know who are they are. What do they do for a living? Who do they know, and how and why are they connected? How long have they known them, how frequently do they interact, and over what types of issues?

What recommendations do they have influence over, and why, so far as you can tell? What perceptions do they seem to have, and do they influence others to form similar views? What decisions do they have authority for and what others do they have some sort of a say over? And, beyond all of this, how do they behave in these conversations?

This is all typically easier to work out where businesses are marketing to other businesses than where a brand is marketing to billions of consumers around the world. The fewer people that are involved in decisions about whether to buy the brand's products or services, the easier it should be, albeit that the buying cycles are normally more complex where more substantial sums of money are involved. Yet with strong data, it is all possible. You just need to know where best to dig, and appreciate that you can't turn over all the topsoil.

Once you've started to work out how influence flows amongst the most influential people in your audience, as a brand you must also face the reality that it's ever-changing. Influence may vary from one scenario or one conversation to another. The personal reputations of those in the mix may change too – for better or worse.

Tapping into influence flows is vital for understanding them though, and for developing standardised approaches for measuring influence. With standardisation, measurement is set to become more clinical. The power of influence can better be charted, and placed in a commercial context.

By understanding not just how people are networked but why they are networked, we can get closer to applying science to the way in which they exert influence. We can begin to measure that influence. And by knowing what buttons we might want to press there, we can make influence a more commercially-tangible component of reputation management.

It brings greater certainty to how the value of influence can be measured, even if reputation, in the hands of the audience, ultimately cannot.

Life in the P&L

But measuring the influence power of networks only goes so far. Public relations cannot be measured clinically across the broad gamut of its influence over reputation. The direct commercial impact of every project budget spent on managing reputation cannot be quantified, although some form of monetary measurement of public relations spend versus reputation change versus commercial outcome is on the horizon.

That's real progress, but it's unlikely to make an accountant smile. Where in the P&L should all of this investment sit, given that while it's becoming more tangible it has historically lumbered uncomfortably as a series of line items in the cost centre of the marketing budget?

Actually, that really doesn't matter. Well it might matter to accountants, for the purpose of business administration, but it does not have any real bearing on whether the money spent creates commercial returns for the organisation by furthering reputation. Which begs the question: shouldn't accountants be sorting out the commercial evaluation of public relations, rather than practitioners?

That would seem logical, but realistically it needs to be people with in-depth editorial understanding and the ability to connect editorial outcomes to business outcomes who sort this out. Only then will we be able to explain to financial teams the variances and data that are factors of modern public relations, and to what extent it is – and isn't – possible to compute the financial value of a brand's reputation. And what part public relations has to play in that.

Social media has brought sweeping changes to the editorial world, but has also had a profound impact on advertising, and indeed in marketing generally. It makes it far more difficult to figure out where one traditional marketing discipline begins and another ends – cue most agencies making attempts to muscle in on area that they previously had no real interest in, with mixed results. Those are growing pains that can cause both opportunity and irritation for agencies, and a fog for marketing departments considering using their services. Yet this has had one substantial benefit – it has made marketers realise that better results and better commercial returns, truly do come when different disciplines either work hand in hand or join to form a single discipline, drawing on the skills of several areas.

Which makes assessment of what truly influences reputation tricky. Public relations has never had the lone bearing on reputation, but in today's more demanding consumer society, in which expectations of brands have increased and there are more points of interface, the whole lifecycle of customer management can influence reputation. Public relations is often left to do what it can to help, or to pick up the pieces. Moreover, as the lines between marketing disciplines blur, it is far more difficult to pick apart which aspects of marketing spend influence reputation, and to what extent. Public relations may be the mainstay, but no longer holds exclusive sway, which makes it impossible to discern PR-driven reputation gains from those achieved by other marketing activities when assessing return on investment.

So where does that leave us, given we need to find some way to make sense of this both for the board and for the accountants? Well, time will tell: commercially-satisfactory evaluation of public relations investment in managing reputation remains a work in progress. Digitising media has put it in close reach but has also further muddied the waters. But one conclusion that does shine through is that no single model will be able to measure business outcomes in monetary terms *and* place measurable commercial value on a brand's reputation.

And someone needs to pay for it.

Francis Ingham, director general of the Public Relations Consultants Association (PRCA), believes that evaluation needs far more focus as public relations becomes more sophisticated. 'The biggest gap we have in public relations at the moment is the need to be able to evaluate our work better. We have to have standard metrics. The problem is that clients don't want to pay for it up front,' he say.

'Tracking activity against sales is one thing, but changes in attitude and behaviour are a different thing. That's right at the heart of the challenge, and we need to find an answer. The key thing though is the approach to evaluation has to be determined right at the beginning of the process,' he adds.

So PR's efforts to measure reputation should probably pursue two avenues, albeit in close alignment. At the same time as piecing together the information feeds that will allow public relations impact to be better assessed by financial outcomes, we should be working with all other marketing disciplines to ensure that reputation measurement is a primary consideration of a more astute, transparent and agile framework for measuring all marketing returns on investment.

Once you've measured, what then?

PR measurement is not easy; in fact it's getting more difficult and yet must be tackled properly if brands are to be able to justify the correlation between money spent managing reputation by influencing editorial and the actual commercial impact of the activity. But with an effective measurement system in place, with as much sophistication as possible built in to meet the needs of the business, what should the next steps be for brands wanting to drive commercial advantage through reputation, and wanting to gain greater returns from their investments in PR?

Before they can drive returns, they should first understand that the only way public relations will become a true asset for them today is to first gain some editorial command for the brand. Not control, because brands cannot control the media today – no one truly can. But by taking the kinds of steps covered in the previous chapters, they can at least seek to command their brand reputations by doing as much as is possible to influence them.

Once they have exercised a degree of command and have systemised a more sophisticated and more agile approach to reputation management, they can then adopt an all-seeing approach to measurement in order to both assess the financial performance of investments in reputation and improve their approach to managing it. This needs a dual approach of both clinically measuring investments against the money that results from them, and assessing the overall value of reputation to the business, albeit without the ability to put pounds and pence against it.

Overall, the value of more accurate and more commercially-savvy public relations measurement to the business is lessened or nullified unless brand managers and those who make the ultimate financial decisions keep clear heads on what they're actually trying to achieve in the reputation game. All the data and all the science in the world are practically worthless unless common sense is used to make the right decisions in order to build a better reputation for the business.

You must know what it is of greatest commercial value for you to measure, then apply the right tools to doing that, in so far as it is currently practical and with your eyes open to how those techniques may improve in the future.

Summary
- The public relations industry has been obsessed with counting things so that the volume of output can be assessed.
- But that doesn't really tell you whether what has been invested in managing reputation is having the desired effect for the organisation. It doesn't correlate with the degree of influence exerted.
- Search technology makes this even more complicated, as perception can be formed and judgements made on the basis

of a mechanistic evaluation of relevance, and even of reputation.

- The public relations industry is responding with initiatives to modernise measurement to increase its commercial relevancy.
- Absolute clinical measurement of reputation is impossible, but measurement of influence is becoming far sharper.
- What can brands learn from measurement in order to gain reputational edge?

CHAPTER

9

PARTICIPATION: THE FUTURE OF ORGANISATIONAL COMMUNICATION

The future of corporate communication lies in a return to public relations: two-way engagement with people and markets. #brandanarchy

By now you should be convinced of the fact that organisations have lost control of their reputations forever. The issue of how to deal with the situation, however, remains. The leadership and vision provided by early professionals has since been squandered. In *Two-Way Street*, published in 1948[1], Eric Goldman describes the three stages of the development of corporate communication during the period from 1900 to the time of the publication of his book:

1. Public fooled via spin
2. Information through communication
3. Public engagement via two-way engagement

It's uncanny how these same stages can just as easily be applied to the public relations industry in the second half of the 20th century. But we're not claiming to be original thinkers in recognising the relevance of these staging posts to the developing public relations industry; the subject has exercised generations of public relations academics.

---

1   Goldman, Eric. *Two-way Street*. Bellman Publishing Company, 1948.

Shortly after the publication of Goldman's book the public relations industry became obsessed about communicating with the public via the proxy of media relations rather than direct public engagement. David Phillips, a public relations practitioner and academic, says that the rise of mass media and its ability to provide a shortcut to large audiences for the change in style of corporate communications: 'In 1962 the Pilkington Report recommended a second BBC channel, a separate service for Wales, and the restructuring of ITV. Transatlantic television became possible. At the same time, the ability to print fast and cheaply brought a concurrent revolution. Public relations had to change and the easy, but not nearly as effective, form of public relations was to use the fast-growing media. It was a communication revolution. The growth of consumer and trade titles in the 1970s saw corporate communication from community influence to print editorial. By 1980 it was dead easy,' he says.

Back to the street

Now that print media is in decline and the Internet has enabled communication with audiences directly via digital media and, ultimately, direct participation within communities, the public relations industry is attempting to modernise and reinvent itself. Phillips believes the industry faces a dramatic upheaval. 'Too often in practice we've confused public relations for media relations,' says Phillips.

Shedding the shackle of media relations will be critical to the future success of the public relations industry. It is inevitable that as traditional media continues to fragment because of technological change, and consumer behaviour becomes increasingly participatory, that organisations must change how they communicate.

Organisations are recognising the opportunity to communicate directly with audiences. But for many organisations this involves simply disseminating content via newswires, websites and Twitter feeds; 'a means of dumping messages', as Grunig describes. The cocktail of print media decline and Internet-enable consumer empowerment means that consumers are open about their likes and dislikes and are quick to vent their frustration at brands via networks such as Facebook, Google + and Twitter. They cannot, and should not, be ignored. The future of communication between an organisation and its audiences must be participative.

The writing is on the wall, and more than likely it is a Facebook wall. Brands that fail to engage with their audiences are on a path to self-destruction. Any gap between a customer's expectation of your product and its reality will drive a conversation on the social web. The evidence is scattered across the Internet for search engines to uncover. According to a report published by Alterian called 'Your Brand: At Risk or Ready for Growth'[2], only five per cent of consumers believe what a company says about itself, whereas a third of respondents using social media believe that companies are genuinely interested in them. And that figure is growing. The study, undertaken in the UK and the United States, found that broadcast marketing is broken; it is too east for consumers to ignore brands. It concludes that companies must rediscover how to engage with consumers. Alterian neatly sums up the three key principles of social media marketing:

1. Analytics to deliver insight
2. Conversational engagement
3. An agile approach to managing and responding to feedback

---

2 Your Brand: At Risk or Ready for Growth?, Alterian www.alterian.com/resource-links/campaigns/brandsatrisk/brands-at-risk

Surveys are typically used as a tool to support a company's own public relations agenda. But Alterian's report, based on qualitative and quantitative research, was written by Professor Michael Hulme, an academic at Lancaster University, and speaks to anyone who is concerned about the reputation of an organisation. Businesses need to redirect marketing spend into audience insight in order to understand and engage with customers as individuals, says Alterian in the report. This requires an investment in skills to retrain the marketing department.

'Meeting the challenge of individualisation will require new thinking in the collection of customer information/data for an organisation to be able to interact at a personal level. This will call for a commitment from the business to both structural and skill changes, arising from the need to break down silos, both departmentally and functionally, to address the "single view" of information but to also understand how the information is being used at any one time across the organisation,' says Professor Hulme.

Searching for answers

To be fair, the public relations industry isn't alone in ignoring lessons from the past. The search marketing industry is no different. In the last five to 10 years digital marketing has reached a place where keywords and inbound links assume more importance on a website than the actual content and audience. But here too a subtle shift is taking place, as media consumption and buying habits are turning to social media. Here, reputation is built and products and services are sold through word of mouth, not purely via search.

Web spam is the issue. We've become so obsessed with search marketing that we've filled the web with useless content in a bid to manipulate search engine results. Search engine marketing has become mechanised to such a point that we've boiled down our audience to keywords. And in this world, the organisation with the largest search budget and the smartest agency wins. We're in danger of taking our eye off the audience and forgetting that it's great content, rather than keywords and links, that build engagement and trust over the long term. Best-practice search marketing is smart but filling the Internet with low-value content isn't. We'll almost certainly come to see the floatation of content development company Demand Media in January 2011[3], with a valuation of $1.5 billion, as the high water mark of search marketing. It generates 7,000 articles a day and has a simple formula: create lots niche content targeted at search engines and generate revenue through ads.

If you want more evidence, look no further than the results from an informational search rather than a commercial search. If you search for information on a topic such as prostate cancer, the results from a search engine will be incredibly useful. But commercial searches are almost always polluted and the site with the biggest budget rises to the top. Search for popular keywords such as 'car insurance', 'holidays' or 'coffee machines' and you'll see what's happening for yourself: highly competitive markets for pay-per-click and millions of natural results packed with web spam. Paid-for search has become more sophisticated and you can become more selective about where you place your ads, but for organic search we're surely close to game over.

Our view is that search will give way to social networks as a means of discovery. It's already happening. In the last five years we've seen the rise of social networks such as Facebook

---

3 Demand Media, Inc. announces the closing of its Initial Public Offering, Demand Media: http://ir.demandmedia.com/phoenix.zhtml?c=215358&p=irol-newsArticle&ID=1521835&highlight=

and Twitter. But there are lots of others focused on niche communities. These are built from trusted friends; friends who understand our personal motivations. We're entering a new era of digital media: the discovery of brands and products through the recommendation of friends in our networks who share links.

You build reputation and sell in this market through word-of-mouth. That means you need to have a deep understanding of your audience. And create compelling content that gets their attention. We're reverting to community life. If the pub provides a lousy meal or bad service, everyone in the village knows about it. But in the contemporary analogy, thanks to the web, the village is now your network on Facebook, Google+ or Twitter. Your organisation needs to have a presence on the web that potential customers can visit but it also needs to have a presence where your audience is, and where conversations are taking place about your organisation and its peers. You need to identify your audience and work out what, editorially, will get its attention. And then you need to inspire people to talk about, listen to and share information about your brand.

Search results for popular terms within social networks are completely unsatisfactory. A timeline of scrolling tweets, riddled with spam, isn't really that helpful. But what about if you overlaid your own network on this set of results and those results were filtered based on the authority of the people you trusted? Bing is incorporating Facebook 'like' into its search algorithms. Google is doing the same with Google+. In future, when you search for a film or restaurant, the results will be prioritised according to the opinions of people in your network. You'll find the Facebook 'like' button on more than two million websites. And at the last count there were more than 500 million people on Facebook including 30 million in the UK. This is the future of search marketing and it mirrors our changing habits of media consumption. Social media types talk of the death of search marketing. That's an overly dramatic stance, of course. Online search isn't going anywhere. But the balance of power will start to shift from search marketing to social media optimisation.

Social relationship management

An inevitable development for the future of social media marketing is to connect social media monitoring systems with customer data within an organisation. This enables data from social media platforms to be incorporated into customer relationship management (CRM) systems. This is an area that PeopleBrowsr UK CEO, Andrew Grill[4], an active social media user and thought leader, has already explored. The problem is that organisations aren't ready.

'CRM systems sometimes don't even have an email address field. The challenge for anyone that runs a CRM system is to add a field that records a customer's social media name (whether it be a Twitter name, Facebook name or a URL) by which the customer can be identified. I have never had a company ask me for my Twitter name, however, I'm easy to guess – @andrewgrill. But if you're @wadds or @mynameisearl, and you are a high-value Vodafone customer tweeting about a problem, how does the customer service team know whether or not to step in?' says Grill.

Grill is frequently vocal on Twitter about service from organisations such as BT, Starbucks and Vodafone. He no longer picks up the phone when he has an issue with an organisation. Instead he sends a Tweet, preferring the asynchronous nature

---

4 Andrew Grill personal website: www.andrewgrill.com. You can follow Andrew on Twitter @andrewgrill

and not having to stay on hold to a call centre. Instead, the companies call him. 'My profile on the BT CRM system does not have my Twitter name but I'm sure I'm on the hotlist of the team that runs the Twitter account in Northern Ireland,' says Grill. While social media has yet to be integrated directly with social media platforms, it is entirely conceivable that measurement tools such as Klout and PeerIndex enable brands to determine the influence of a Twitter user and prioritise their response accordingly.

Escherman's Andrew Smith shares that view. 'For big organisations and brands, the sheer volume of customer interactions they have to deal with means that they're going to use shortcuts in order to prioritise their customer service response. For example, an unhappy customer with a PeerIndex score of 60 is going to get prioritised over someone with a score of 20. You may say that's unfair but that's the reality of the world we live in,' says Smith.

Perhaps the first indication that organisations are seriously tooling up to integrate social media beyond marketing, and into their customer relationship management systems, came in March 2010 when business software firm Salesforce acquired social media monitoring firm Radian6. Salesforce.com already had some basic social monitoring and analytics capability but Radian6 will enable it to enhance its capability for brand management and monitoring and, crucially, the emerging areas of social sales and CRM. Salesforce.com has said that it is integrating Radian6 into three areas of its business, namely customer engagement via social media with the Sales and Service Cloud, reputation monitoring with Salesforce Chatter and integrating social features into the Force.com platform so that developers are able to put the social web into everything they build.

So is engaging via Twitter a cure-all for customer service woes? In our opinion, no, but even if it is, it is going to take a generation before Twitter is adopted as a customer service channel. It's a start, however, and is a way for brands to further understand the needs of a customer and take action.

What could be clearer than a customer telling you what they want? For now, Twitter is a tax that companies must accept as a cost of providing poor products or service. We're only beginning to see the use of Twitter for customer service. But the expectation of brands that use the channel is increasing all the time. Ultimately, the ability for consumers to communicate directly with organisations is likely to require fundamental corporate and organisational change.

Social media and communication in a crisis

We couldn't write a book on the future of organisational communication without a comment on the impact of the Internet and social media on crisis communication. Principally, the impact is two-fold: speed and participation. Technology enables a crisis to be communicated at breakneck speed and social media enables anyone to comment on it. A situation that starts as a tweet can quickly spread via networks. It will typically be amplified and inflamed as it spreads. But corporate communicators are better armed than ever before to deal with a crisis situation as it arises. The social web allows every conversation to be monitored in real time. You might not like the fact that conversations that are taking place publicly about you but at least you have the opportunity to listen in and, crucially, take appropriate action.

'The rise of social media has forever altered the corporate reputational landscape. Individuals and NGOs alike enjoy unprecedented access and reach within an increasingly diversified digital media space; one in which everyone is an expert and a publisher. The transition to [the social web] has brought with it an array of associated reputational risks and opportunities which modern organisations need to understand

and acknowledge as part of their crisis planning and management activities,' says Michael Regester, founding director of Regester Larkin.

Prior to 2000, a crisis communication situation was led by broadcast; either radio or television news. It had both the audience and the airtime to play out a story in real time. Newsprint, with its 24-hour cycle, followed with deeper analysis. Now, people at the scene share the news loaded with their own comment and opinion.

'Social media can trigger and escalate a problem or crisis. It is not only commercial organisations that break news. Damaging information increasingly enters the public domain via a range of social media platforms including Twitter, YouTube, Wikipedia and citizen journalist websites and blogs. It can also serve to magnify and perpetuate an issue that may otherwise, due to factors such as commercial news values and other practical and resource constraints, have faded from public view. In this sense, in some instances, social media itself can become the problem,' adds Regester.

Whatever the pace of a crisis event, the nature of it, or the media by which it breaks, the response effort should follow best practice. That means preparing for an event long before it breaks out by scenario planning and rehearsing crisis events. In their excellent handbook to crisis communication, *Risk Issues and Crisis Management in Public Relations*[5], Michael Regester and Judy Larkin summarise the key components of a crisis communication plan:

1. Develop a positive attitude towards crisis management

---

5   Regester, Michael, and Larkin, Judy. *Risk Issues and Crisis Management in Public Relations*. Kogan Page, 2010.

2. Bring the organisation's performance into line with public expectation
3. Build credibility through a succession of responsible deeds
4. Be prepared to act on opportunities during a crisis
5. Appoint appropriate teams to act on opportunities during a crisis
6. Catalogue potential crisis situations and devise policies for their prevention
7. Put the plan in writing
8. Test, test and test again

We've already heard from Dominic Burch and his communications team at Walmart-owned Asda headquartered in Leeds, UK. He has more than 15 years' experience in frontline corporate communications but it is in his role at Asda that he has faced his most testing crisis situations. His responses have been textbook stuff. In 2009, the police launched an investigation at Asda's request into a supermarket worker who called himself Adeel Ayub. The employee had previously (three years earlier) been based at a store in Fulwood, Lancashire but had since left the business. However mobile phone content had been posted to YouTube now that showed him urinating in a bin, playing cricket with food items and wreaking havoc in the aisles during night shifts three years previously. He was also observed slashing the coats of other employees and breaking furniture in the staffroom.

Management at the store were aware of instances of vandalism at the time, but not the culprit. There was also footage of Ayub setting off fire alarms and the resulting response from firefighters. The most disgusting footage showed him ripping the wrapper from a chicken and apparently licking it before returning it to the refrigeration cabinet. It resulted in the tabloid media labelling him the 'Asda chicken licker'. Asda's response, led by the in-house communications team, was to acknowledge the situation and assure the media and customers that the rogue employee no longer worked for Asda.

But Asda went further, with the communications team heading down to the Fulwood store to capture the thoughts of staff who had worked with Ayub on the same nightshift, and to interview the store manager in person. They invited them to speak to camera about their former colleague. The results make for powerful viewing. 'One by one Ayub's colleagues gave their response to the actions of their former colleague. Each interview told a powerful story of frustration and disappointment,' said Burch. This first-hand storytelling was more powerful than any traditional corporate response could possibly ever have been. It was authentic and transparent. We posted it to all YouTube and as a result it got 3,500 hits in the first week, so almost one in three people who witnessed the original video saw our colleagues' response. As a result both the media and customer reaction was fairly neutral. Their criticism was focused at the childish actions of Ayub, not toward Asda as a supermarket or employer.

Brands as media

As the fragmentation of media continues apace, organisations are creating their own media products. Blogs are the best example of this medium but Twitter feeds, LinkedIn groups and YouTube channels are also examples of platforms on which companies generate their own content and share it directly with their audiences as a means of engagement. Branded media content is a step along the route to two-way communication, or conversation, to adopt social media parlance. Instead of pushing press releases as the primary means of communication, public relations teams turn publisher and tell stories on behalf of an organisation. The tone is intended to be less corporate and more human. Individuals take the role of journalists and use text, images and video to tell the stories of an organisation to its audience.

In 2005, a *BusinessWeek* cover story announced that a revolution was set to sweep through corporate communications. Public relations and communications teams would cease to exist as business leaders used the web to communicate directly with their audiences. Blogs promised to fundamentally change the relationship between a company and its staff, customers, suppliers and the media. Websites would be overhauled for the 2.0 era, the press release would cease to exist and the public relations industry itself faced revolution. We're still waiting. It's an overstatement of the case, of course, but six years on there are very few examples of large UK organisations – outside the media and information industries – that have successfully used a blog as the centrepiece of their communications strategy.

Yet the benefits of corporate blogging are undisputed: direct engagement, leadership, search marketing, social capital and raw web traffic. As a rule, good corporate blogs are hard to find. And for every success, the Internet is littered with the twitching corpses of dormant corporate blogs. They started with a burst of regular posts but enthusiasm waned as the posts failed to engage with their intended audience and, inevitably, the posts became less frequent and, in time, completely dried up.

One of the reasons that there are so few examples of good corporate blogs is because of the clash between personal and corporate communication. There are fundamental differences between how people communicate and how companies communicate – and very few corporate organisations have managed to bridge that gap.

Then there is the issue of ownership. Should a blog be the pet project of a senior executive or fall within the communications, public relations, product marketing, customer relations or human resources teams? And the legal arm of any organisation will almost certainly want to get involved and pass judgement on blog posts and comments. Finally, there is the issue of the generation of authentic content. It's the only way to attract and stimulate an audience yet organisations see it as time-consuming and requiring the constant input of senior management.

Bridges don't talk; people do

Shifting from traditional forms of corporate communication to social communication necessitates a change of language that not all organisations are able to make. The language of the social web is familiar and friendly. It's the antithesis of most corporate communication. It's authentic. The @towerbridge Twitter account provides a great case study that spotlights exactly this issue. It was originally set up in 2008 when Twitter was less than a couple of years old. The account provided witty updates about traffic on the River Thames in London when the iconic bridge opened and closed as boats passed up and down the river. It was the brainchild of Tom Armitage, a games designer who operated the account independently of the owners of the bridge. It was a simple commentary on a London landmark that was followed by 4,000 people and regularly received mainstream media attention. Then in May 2010, @towerbridge abruptly announced: 'Hi – we're new to Twitter. Follow us to find out what's happening in and around Tower Bridge. Did you know there's an exhibition inside?' The account had been claimed by its rightful owner who had eliminated its irreverent history. Fair enough; but to ignore Armitage's obvious success and erase his good work as the prior voice of the account was a tactical mistake.

Participation

In time, perhaps, we'll see the death of the website as a marketing vehicle. If your audience is interacting on the social web, why would you create a website elsewhere on the Internet? This is a tactic that organisations are testing. You'll struggle to find a website promoting Talisker, the whisky from Skye in Scotland, owned by Diageo; but head to Facebook and search for Talisker and you'll soon discover it, along with 140,000 other proponents of the brand. Here you'll discover photos from the distillery, competitions and details of tasting events, alongside the comments of lots of engaged Talisker fans.

But this sort or participatory engagement isn't just limited to consumer brands. Social networking is increasingly being used by public sector organisations to reach their citizens. Northumberland County Council faces a unique challenge in communicating with its 300,000 citizens that are spread over 160 square miles, often in remote rural locations.

During the hard winter of 2010, it used a Facebook page to alert residents to road and school closures. The engagement on this page, combined with research that showed that more than 50 per cent of residents are active on Facebook, prompted Northumberland County Council to extend its strategy to include events pages that enable residents to sign up to and be alerted about everything from the summer reading challenge at local libraries to big events at National Trust attractions.

Developing communities

Savvy organisations are starting to harness the conversations that are taking place about them, or with relevance to them, to develop their own managed communities. When former Virgin communications chief Will Whitehorn was leading the Virgin Galactic project, he used an early form of social media to build a community of customers for the visionary space project. Virgin Galactic was created in 2004 to sell the promise of space tourism and a ride on the first commercial spacecraft. Whitehorn steered Virgin Galactic from concept to reality, convincing investors, overseeing technical plans and moving to a position where daily flights to 100 miles above the Earth's surface have become possible. 'The first six months in the job was spent trying to find 100 high net worth customers willing to pay $200,000 for a trip into space. We told a story and sold a dream using public relations as our single means of marketing. We generated attention by creating big events around key milestones such as test flights and by enabling journalists and bloggers to share the experience,' says Whitehorn.

Virgin Galactic now has more than 400 customers waiting to take a three-minute flight into space in 2012 when the spacecraft is due to launch. Before then, customers have the opportunity to speak to each other via what is surely must be the world's most exclusive online social network – Space Book. 'Facebook launched in 2004. We came up with Space Book before we'd even heard of Facebook. We launched the Virgin Galactic website with a community for our future astronauts. It enables customers to talk to each other and share their views. At the same time, the Galactic team gets the opportunity to understand the concerns and motivations of its customers,' adds Whitehorn.

Developing a social media strategy

Social media requires input from all levels in an organisation and is likely to lead to the restructuring of many of the operational parts of the corporate organisation as it integrates social media into marketing, customer relationship management, sales and even product development. You can almost smell the panic as organisations recognise that their audience is shifting its attention from conventional mainstream media to social media. According to David Cushman, managing director and co-founder of international open business consultancy, 90:10 Group, there are two possible reactions: some organisations view social media as a bolt-on channel to traditional methods of communicating with an audience, while others see it as a strategic platform for customer engagement.

In utilising social media as a bolt-on channel, an organisation transfers the communication techniques that it has used with its traditional audiences, typically the media, and supplements them with a sprinkling of social media workings. You can spot these organisations every day on Twitter, spewing out content with little or no audience engagement. The strategic approach to social media recognises, and tries to capitalise on, the opportunity that social media offers: to put its customers at its heart. That process starts with researching the conversations that are already taking place around an organisation and its markets, and move on to the development of a strategic communications plan, anchored around suitable content, to assess the opportunity for the organisation to help build and participate in this newly emerging approach to audience relations.

'The senior managers within customer-centric organisations increasingly recognise that social media is hugely positive. I think we've passed the moment where managers are asking about the value of social media. The opportunity to engage with customers in a participatory medium is transformational,' says Cushman.

The shift to open business

90:10 has developed a strategy called 'open business' to describe the future of a business that participates with its audiences via social media. These are shared enterprises that are constructed to create best-fit outcomes for the actual, rather than perceived, needs of their customers. 'They engage with their customers and potential customers with a view to insight, innovation and change. Their role is to be the 10 per cent discovering those who share their purpose, bringing them together, surfacing their needs and then enabling, supporting and delivering innovations against the expressed needs of the 90 per cent,' says Cushman. According to Cushman, the start of the journey towards being an open business requires the development of evidence- and insight-based strategic approaches based on four areas:

1. Understand the community landscape in which you operate
2. Clarify the needs, abilities and attitudes of customers, staff, senior teams and other stakeholders, in respect of social media and its technology
3. Identify what needs to change about crisis management and decision-making processes
4. Learn how the organisation functions and how data flows through it

'Learning from each step we can build an organisation that embraces social media and is ready to take full advantage of the opportunities offered to open businesses. One thing is certain; the organisation which derives value from its connection to its customers is going to outperform those that don't. And those organisations which quickly learn how to do that best are going to be first to the top,' says Cushman.

Mark Adams, partner and chief operating officer of the Conversation Group, believes that the catalyst for change in organisations comes from one of two places. He believes that we're at a melting point where both conventional and social media co-exist – but not for much longer.

'Change in an organisation is typically being driven by an enthusiastic individual that is evangelical about the potential of social media technologies, often surrounded by sceptics concerned with security and governance; or it's the realisation by executives that the Internet is changing how customers and employees buy and engage with an organisation,' he says. In organisations that are engaged in social media, programmes are usually piloted by marketing or communications teams. According to Adams, gains are expected or anticipated but frequently not achieved because of the latent inertia of the organisation.

'They will have started using some new social media tool, maybe an internal social network or an external Twitter account, and maybe an employee collaboration tool. They will almost certainly be in breach of company policies since legal protection typically lags behind the use of social media tools,' says Adams. If individuals within an organisation fail to persuade executives of the importance of social media, in time the market almost certainly will. Adams compares top-line sales growth with the performance of online and traditional sales to predict when an organisation will cross a threshold of 50 per cent of sales online. At that point he says it will become

When does a firm become an 'Online Firm'?

(When the majority of its revenue comes from online)

Total revenue:	**500**
Annual growth rate of total from online:	**5.00%**
Share of revenues today from online:	**20.00%**
Growth rate of online revenues:	**25.00%**
The firm become an online firm on:	**02 January 2016**

Figure: When does a firm become an online firm? (Source: Mark Adams, The Conversation Group)

an online organisation, and for most organisations that date is approaching within the next five to 10 years.

'If you are a retailer or manufacturer and your revenues grow predictably by five per cent each year and 20 per cent of your revenues are from online sales today but they are growing by 25 per cent each year, by January 2016, the majority of your organisation's revenues will come from online sources. Around this time, the firm will need to be thinking and acting like an online firm,' says Adams.

The second shift in organisations is a social one. According to Adams, when more than 50 per cent of an organisation's employees are on Facebook and able to talk about their workplace, the boundaries between corporate and personal life will cease to exist. 'People have emotions, attitudes and opinions. They used to be largely private matters, or shared with friends. Now at a click of a button they are public. This has created a new wave of social behaviours, engaging people in their personal life and the workplace,' says Adams.

This shift will strike at the core of corporate communications and human resources. Conversations in the office will continue at home and vice versa. The change from businesses organised by command and control to enterprises that are open and engaged with their audiences will be an evolution and not a revolution, says Adams: 'Companies want quick change and aren't used to scaling up processes. Control pervades. But we don't know what the future looks like and the best approach is to acknowledge uncertainty and turn the protectionism of organisations into a religion.'

Both Cushman and Adams describe an environment in which everyone in an organisation has a communications role. That means radical change for anyone who currently develops a communications strategy on behalf of a business or has a role in executing that strategy. But it also means that anyone within an organisation will need to be able to communicate on behalf of the brand and fully understand their role in building its reputation.

It's called participation.

Summary

- The public relations industry is attempting to modernise as media declines and digital media enables organisations to participate with their communities.
- Organisations are recognising the opportunity to communicate directly with markets, but organisations typically broadcast their content to their audience rather than attempting to engage.
- Search market is set to give way to discovery via social networks. In the future search engines will be overlaid on social networks.
- Social networks enable a crisis situation to be monitored at grassroots level before if breaks.
- Anyone can share and comment on an organisation involved in a crisis. But proven techniques for dealing with a crisis situation hold up.
- Shifting from traditional forms of corporate communication to social forms of communication requires a change in style and tempo of language.
- In time social media will impact all the operational areas of an organisation, requiring the organisation and its employees, to participate with its communities.

CHAPTER

10

RESKILLING FOR THE FUTURE

The marketing, media and public relations industries are
modernising. But are you and your organisation?
#brandanarchy

The public relations industry is enjoying a renaissance.
Conventional media is fragmenting and social networks are
connecting organisations and their audiences in a direct
relationship. The editorial, influence and engagement skills of
the public relations industry mean that it has a crucial role at
the heart of these changes. There has arguably never been a
more exciting time to work in the industry. But it's also
incredibly daunting. Practitioners must learn new skills and
expertise if they want to have a future in the industry.

The big modernisation challenge

People starting out in their careers today are likely to see the
biggest changes in the media that we have ever seen, probably
since the invention of the printing press around 1440.
Modernisation is the biggest issue that the public relations
industry needs to face up to. That's not only our view but is
shared by almost everyone that we've spoken to during the
development of this book. The public relations industry is locked
into a workflow that has its origins in the 1950s. If the industry is
to develop, that has to change. The public relations industry has
already missed out on the opportunity created by the emergence
of the search marketing industry and a new breed of agency has
emerged to pick up the work. The same may yet happen with the
opportunity presented by social media.

The industry faces a mixture of fear and entrenched practices.
Yet despite all the talk about moving into a new age and

adopting new skills, the number one thing people are still doing in the public relations industry is media relations. We caught up with Andrew Smith of Escherman and asked him about his experience as a trainer for the Chartered Institute of Public Relations (CIPR), the UK's professional body for public relations industry, and the Public Relations Consultants Association (PRCA), the UK trade association. 'I delivered a session at the CIPR last March and there were about 70 senior communication directors in attendance. I asked them how many of them utilised data from Google Analytics to inform their approaches to communication planning and not a single hand went up. That's shameful, when you think of the extraordinary amount of data information that is freely available to help determine and shape what communication strategies are more likely to work,' he says.

'Yet calling journalists and asking "did you get my press release?" continues to be the primary activity that public relations agencies and in-house communication functions are still primarily geared around. It's going to take time to crack and it's going to take people to make a real effort to break away from that mindset. There may be pure media relations opportunities for some very niche operators out there but they are going to be fewer and farther between,' adds Smith.

As Smith spotlights, the industry is at a crossroads although it is almost certainly in denial. The Internet has dealt a brutal blow to the media and it is in a process of reinventing itself. For now, media relations continues to be an important part of managing the reputation of an organisation. But new influencers such as bloggers and Twitter users, with a high level of authority on a relevant topic, must also be considered as part of the communication mix, as should communities in which conversations are taking place about organisations with or without their involvement. Inevitably, over time, media relations will become a smaller element of reputation management and the emerging areas will come to dominate. You must put yourself in the best possible position to operate in this new environment.

Communication skills for the future

Practitioners must first and foremost recognise how technology is impacting upon the media, how it is enabling brands to develop their own content and forms of media, and how networks and communities develop and operate online. This is an essential step to recognising the skills required to operate in this new environment. In the table below we've returned to some of the key trends explored in this book and have identified what personal skills practitioners require in order to meet the challenges.

Trend	Description	Skills
Branded media	As media fragments, organisations are creating their own media products. Organisations are now media owners in their own right. Blogs are the best example of this medium but Twitter feeds, LinkedIn groups and YouTube channels are also examples of platforms companies use to generate their own content and share it directly with their audiences as a means of engagement.	Creativity and editorial skills are required to develop compelling content that engages the target audience.

Trend	Description	Skills
Engagement and conversation	Conversations are almost certainly taking place about your organisation in online communities scattered across the Internet, whether you like it or not. Your organisation needs to monitor these exchanges and determine whether not it has a role to contribute. There is also an opportunity for your organisation to develop communities of its own, both internally and externally, to engage with staff, customers, prospects, and other stakeholders. Online conversation is a two-way process, typically in real time. In the same way that individuals interact with each other the expectation in the social web is that companies should respond to their customers in a timely fashion, using an appropriate tone of voice.	Good interpersonal and social skills are essential to represent a brand and be its voice online.
Speed	Digital communication removes the print media constraints of page space and deadline. News stories are written and published in real time. Spokespeople need to be available on demand and content must be supplied to tight deadlines. Any delay will mean you miss out. The same rule applies in direct communication between a company and its audience. Misinformation can quickly escalate into a crisis online.	Interaction and communication on the web requires a level-headed attitude. Individuals must be calm and considered.

Trend	Description	Skills
Planning	PR and media relations have been clumsily interchanged during the past two decades. Audience planning has been limited to looking up a media category in a directory rather than thoroughly researching an audience segment and analysing its influences. That's changing. Planning tools such as Google Insights allow practitioners to gain sophisticated intelligence about audiences and their motivations that can be used as the basis for campaign planning.	Rudimentary mathematics and a familiarity with analytics are increasingly important for practitioners in the development, implementation and measurement of campaigns.
Monitoring	The press clipping book is dead. Companies need real-time data to enable them to respond and adapt programmes in real time as they are being implemented. The feedback loop should be hours, not weeks. Real-time monitoring combined with editorial nous makes this a reality.	The Internet doesn't have an 'off' button. Business online is relentless. Attention to detail and quick-wittedness are required.
Integration	Social media democratises communication. Functional departments within organisations must work together because customers expect it. A Facebook page set up as a brand fan page is just as likely to be used as a customer service or sales channel as a Twitter feed used to push out corporate content. Companies must have clear processes for signposting conversations to customer service, public relations and sales.	Practitioners must be familiar with all aspects of the business and be able to work across functional departments within an organisation.

Trend	Description	Skills
Measurement	The public relations and communication industry is growing wiser and has rightly cast aside AVEs and has recognised that the industry should measure outcomes not outputs. AMEC is working on a new measurement framework. In the interim the PRSA has proposed the so-called 'Valid Metrics' framework which aligns the workflow of a public relations campaign. Philip Sheldrake has proposed the Influence Scorecard as a means of tracking key performance indicators within an organisation that pertain to influence.	As with planning, rudimentary mathematics and a familiarity with analytics is increasingly important in the measurement of campaigns.
Technology	Internet-driven technology is driving the reputation of organisations. Progress is incredibly rapid. Google launched in 1998; Facebook in 2004; and Twitter in 2006. The oldest online 'newspaper', The Telegraph (now telegraph.co.uk), was launched only in 2004. Yet it seems inconceivable that we would operate without any of these services today.	Fearless and a willingness to test new products and applications are critical to anyone wanting to stay ahead.

Table: The skills required for practitioners operating in the new reputation landscape.

Professional development rethink

Basic training in core skills and practice should be the foundation of the industry. Educators must align their teaching with the day-to-day role of a public relations professional, but the industry must also take responsibility for professional development. Public relations educator Richard Bailey[1] has called for the public relations degree to be reinvented. He reckons that degrees could be delivered in two years at the same time as balancing academic theory with practical craft: 'In response to higher university fees, let's offer some genuinely full-time degree courses. These could be delivered in two years. Let's deliver a much slower track to those in full-time work, sponsored by their employers to study part-time. Delivery will have to shift from face-to-face to online learning. The learning will move out of the university and into the workplace. The university becomes a partner in, rather than an owner of, the course,' he says.

We're almost certain that Bailey would have a supporter in his call for a rethink of public relations education in fellow public relations educator and practitioner Heather Yaxley[2]. She says that the industry needs to take responsibility for educating its professionals, citing WPP boss Sir Martin Sorrell's[3] now infamous comment that the industry nicks talent rather than training and developing people in-house.

'There are many ways to learn and develop but the best take effort and investment. Too much training and development in public relations seems to involve attending industry conferences where the pinnacle of learning seems to be listening to other practitioners giving anecdotal reports of their own experiences. Learning is primarily "on the job", often at the hands of those who do little more than pass on poor practices. I believe these

---

1 Richard Bailey blogs at PRStudies: www.prstudies.com/. You can follow him on Twitter: @behindthespin
2 Heather Yaxley blogs at Greenbanana: www.greenbanana.biz/. You can follow her on Twitter @greenbanana
3 Sir Martin Sorrell, CEO, WPP: www.wpp.com/wpp/about/whoweare/leadership.htm#name2

are all areas in which the professional bodies and training organisations need to do more and not simply focus on their revenue generation potential,' she says.

We're not so naive as to think any system is perfect, but in the UK the CIPR has made huge strides in taking its professional development programme scheme[4] online. Participants are required to earn a quota of points per year by participating in training activities or by submitting work for assessment. It's exactly what you'd expect from professions such as finance or law. But Yaxley remains critical. 'I'd like to see training courses include some form of outcome for students so there is genuine learning, not simply attendance. This could be in the form of a post-session online test which confirms learning and turns attending a course into genuine personal development,' she says.

Herein lies the major flaw in debating professional development in the public relations industry. It isn't a profession. It lacks the discipline of professional training, or a requirement for examinations and continuous professional development. At best it's a craft to which the cost of entry is an ability to use a phone and computer. Individuals can gain skills via training or through work experience; they aren't formally tested as a requirement to operate in the industry in the same way that accountants, lawyers and medics must train and pass exams and then undertake rigorous ongoing professional development.

The industry needs to support practitioner development but individuals must also take personal responsibility. 'It is a minority that bother to join a professional body and attend any form of training or development courses, or who sign up for the

---

4 CIPR Continuous Professional Development (CPD) programme: www.cipr.co.uk/content/careers-cpd/about-cpd

qualifications offered by a professional organisation or a post-graduate university qualification. Even fewer are members of a professional development scheme. CPD systems are laudable but they need to be robust and should be compulsory if the professional bodies are serious about development,' says Yaxley.

Successful people, in any field, are those that work hard and make a point of surrounding themselves with other successful people. We're with Malcolm Gladwell[5], author of *Outliers*[6], when he wrote that you need 10,000 hours' experience to become exceptional in any area of expertise. There are no shortcuts. Not even in the public relations industry. The chasm between basic training and expert knowledge in a field requires continuous professional development, training and mentoring. Practitioners and their employers, whether agency or in-house, have a crucial role to play in developing the next generation of public relations practitioners.

Getting ahead

Fortunately, there is no shortage of information or content available for individuals seeking to learn the skills demanded by this new brand reputation landscape. The table on pages 227–230 sets out the areas that we believe are most important. We hope that this book has provided you with a good grounding in many of these areas but to continue the process we'd recommend that you seek out professional organisations such as e-consultancy, the CIPR and the PRCA in the UK, and the Public Relations Society of America (PRSA) in the US, and follow practitioners and educators online. Therein lies a lesson

---

5   Malcolm Gladwell personal website: www.gladwell.com/
6   Gladwell, Malcolm. *Outliers: The Story of Success*. Penguin, 2008.

in itself. The web lowers the cost of access to information and self-education. The sum of all knowledge on any topic, including reputation management, is available online, for anyone equipped with a web browser, to explore and read. And the best bit? In the case of reputation management, the Internet provides access to the tools and networks to explore the potential for developing reputation online.

Journalists often make the best PRs. That's because they understand the editorial process and can craft content that will elicit a positive reaction from an audience. They have been trained in the art of storytelling, too. It's a key skill that everyone operating in the business of reputation needs to learn. But words alone won't do the job. You must understand the community with which you are seeking to engage and the purpose of what you are doing.

Personal education in reputation management should start with Google. After all, it's the place where most journeys on the web start. Almost everyone uses Google as a means of discovery but, as we've heard, many individuals are only just starting to use it to inform online reputation and public relations campaigns. As well as simply using the search engine to discover information about organisations and individuals, you can do an awful lot with Google's free tools. Yet the reputation industry is only just beginning to get to grips with the fact that Google makes all this data available on the web *for free*. It costs absolutely nothing to discover how many people searched for your organisation's name last month, or last year, and what related search terms they used. Head to Google's Keyword Tool[7] and try for yourself – right now. Armed with this information, you can start to generate content that matches the

---

terms for which people are searching. Welcome to the business of search marketing.

The Internet has no respect for traditional business models. Google provides free access to services and information that would have demanded a premium before. If you don't have a Gmail account already, get one right away and start by exploring some of the services. Google Reader is web application for tracking RSS feeds, a distribution format provided by almost all online media outlets. Google Alerts real-time alerts to mentions of a keyword in online publications or blogs. Meanwhile, Google's DoubleClick Ad Planner[8] provides user information for almost any significant website. For example, a search for information about BBC News tells me that: it receives 42 million visitors per month of which 31 million are UK based; 64 per cent of visitors are aged 25 to 44; the male to female split is 64 to 36; and that 72 per cent earn more than £30,000 per annum[9]. Users can map a target audience against a location, demographic and online interest. Google provides these tools primarily to enable advertisers to build campaigns with better reach and relevance but of course they are of huge benefit to the reputation management industry.

Building a network online

If you're making your first foray into social networking, Google + [10] (launched in June 2011) is a good starting point for the simple reason that content featured in your personal profile will be highly discoverable via a Google search. The network is

---

8   DoubleClick Ad Planner: www.google.com/adplanner/
9   Data about news.bbc.co.uk from DoubleClick Ad Planner, September 2011
10 Google+: plus.google.com/

available via the web and there are mobile applications for Android and Apple.

Google + is reckoned to be Google's shot at countering Facebook's dominance in consumer social networking (in 2011, it had 750 million users[11]). Google clearly has its work cut out, particularly as many of the new services remain a work in progress. Their plan is to make all of its applications social, thus enabling you to share information with your network. Google faces an uphill challenge in getting users to shift from Facebook. The driver may be privacy. Facebook has been criticised by users on numerous occasions for not transparently communicating its privacy settings. Facebook's role in enabling you to build your online reputation is limited. It has a huge appeal for consumer organisations seeking to explore, engage and generate conversations related to their business and for this reason you should explore it, but business-to-business audiences are almost certainly likely to be elsewhere on the Internet.

LinkedIn is the grandfather of business-to-business social networks. It enables individuals to build and manage a professional network and create a personal portfolio. Users complete a profile of the workplaces and the people with whom they have worked. You can post updates, information about recent professional assignments and link your profile to other content from around the web. As such, it is a living CV that is searchable via the LinkedIn website, mobile applications and search engines such as Google. It's also a good way of promoting your expertise and finding people that you might want to work with. It is worth paying the monthly subscription fee so that you are able to access data about who has visited your account.

---

11 Facebook Statistics: www.facebook.com/press/info.php?statistics

Armed with this information, you can make a proactive approach to people searching for you or your organisation.

If Facebook is your personal network and LinkedIn your professional network, Twitter is the crossover between the two. It's a place where you can dip in and out and know that there will always be someone with which to exchange a message or two. Networking is an overused and abused phrase but it used to take an individual starting out in their career years to build up a professional network. As journalists, we both spent our fair share of evenings in the pub in a bid to build a contacts book. But that no longer needs to be the case. People throughout your industry are almost certainly on Twitter. We suggest that you go and seek them out and add them to your list of the people you follow. In this sense, Twitter is democratising communication and relationships – you can connect with anyone in your industry and follow their comments. Every day on Twitter you can listen in on conversations taking place between people from all walks of life. Hashtags enable conversations around a particular topic to be tagged and give rise to niche communities in their own right. There will almost certainly be a hashtag for your own area of interest or location. Connect with the two of us (@mynameisearl and @wadds) and track the hashtag #brandanarchy. It's a good place to start out and explore the network.

Personal reputation

Antony Mayfield introduced the concept of a personal web footprint in *Me and My Web Shadow*, his book about managing personal reputation online[12]. Managing your personal web

---

12 Mayfield, Antony. *Me and My Web Shadow: How to Manage Your Reputation Online*. A&C Black Publishers, 2010.

shadow is crucial, says Mayfield, as our lives increasingly move online. It's important for anyone who wants to develop a career in communications as the web is the first place people will look to find out about you. But more than that, Mayfield believes that openness online is rewarded. Developing and managing your web footprint will increase your connections to people and access to opportunities, he says.

Mayfield's personal web shadow extends over his blog and a variety of social networks. Look him up via Google and you'll see the benefit of investing in a web shadow for yourself. In his book, Mayfield focuses on blogs, Facebook, Twitter and LinkedIn as a means of building a personal profile online. Inevitably, the issue arises of how you maintain a presence in so many places and segment each network.

We asked Antony for his personal view.

Blog   'When it comes to the social web, blogging was my first love and it remains one of the most exciting and valuable parts of my working life. Establishing, developing and maintaining a blog requires significantly more effort and time than other elements of maintaining your web shadow, but the rewards are significant. A blog can give you a great deal of control over your web shadow and potential to develop your online presence. You can define its look and feel and pull together all the strands and streams of your different profiles and activities in one place. Search engines love blogs. They have fresh content, are well connected and are can easily be crawled by search engines.'

Facebook 'Facebook is a personal space for me, mainly for friends and family. I restrict what people see about me, and things I post there, beyond that network of people, partly for privacy, but mostly so that I don't have to feel too self-conscious about posting endless updates about family life, running, or whatever, which will be boring, or even irritating, to many people in that volume. Colleagues and acquaintances that I "friend" on Facebook see some content, but not everything – this isn't a business networking space for me. It feels a little harsh dividing people into groups or degrees of closeness, but it is necessary to do so in order to make the network useful for you and them.'

Twitter   'Twitter is a very special network for me. It's mainly for sharing thoughts about what is happening right now and getting those amazing moments of serendipity when someone posts a link or a thought that is precisely relevant to me in that moment. How I manage this network is simple: I follow people who are interesting to me at that time, and unfollow those who seem to be less relevant at the moment. I allow anyone except blatant spammers and bots to follow me (I block them) and try hard not to be offended if they unfollow me – I appreciate that I might not be useful to them right at that moment.'

LinkedIn   'As my blog is my public notebook, LinkedIn is my public contact book, biography and a functional, business networking space. I don't cross-post to Twitter as I don't think most people hang out there like they do on Facebook or Twitter, and the volume of posts would be irritating. I'll connect with anyone who seems interesting and relevant, but mostly people whom I have met. There's no real need to segment networks in this space, beyond giving endorsements only to people I have actually worked with and not connecting with people I have reason not to trust.'

Developing digital expertise and online reputation takes time. It's an issue of which Mayfield is acutely aware. 'Think of social media services like Twitter as productivity enhancers first. Reputation is a byproduct, an outcome, of living and working effectively with the web. There's an investment of time to be made in learning how to use both specific web tools and, more generally, about how to live and work in online networks. Beyond this, the things that enhance your online reputation should be a part of your work. Management consultant and writer John Hagel[13] calls Twitter a serendipity engine – you have more coincidences when you are present in online networks: you hear about that article, that job, that conversation which helps your work, nudges your thinking and your career forward a little,' says Mayfield.

Blogs as a personal brand voice

Having built a profile online and created social networks, you need to start creating content and participating in communities online. A personal blog is one of the most effective ways. Blogs are a means for an individual to create their own media property and comment on issues relevant to their own area of expertise. They also provide a means with which to engage with other bloggers and engage in conversations as issues are debated around the web. Content can be syndicated to other websites, increasing your reach and, if you're blogging regularly on topical issues, it will almost certainly be picked up journalists. Opportunities for media comment, news business and public speaking have all come our way via blogs.

Neville Hobson is a UK-based professional communicator, podcaster and blogger who has built his reputation as a thought leader in the communications industry, thanks largely to blogging and podcasting. He started blogging about communication and technology in 2002. He believes that the main benefit of blogging is building a personal reputation online and getting noticed. 'It's very helpful to have a record of content online that shows up prominently in a search. It has almost certainly resulted in connections and work that wouldn't have come to me in any other way,' says Hobson.

But for Hobson, personal development and skills are equally important outcomes of almost 10 years publicly blogging. 'It has enabled me to develop a voice and build confidence in articulating and developing my thoughts publicly. The almost instantaneous feedback loop and public comments mean that you very quickly develop a thick skin and a confidence in your convictions. It makes you much sharper,' he says.

Perhaps you're not ready for the commitment or public scrutiny of a blog. If not, there are plenty of ways that you can contribute content online that will enable you to build your digital skills and, ultimately, your online reputation. Seek out online publications and communities focused on topics related to your area of expertise and start to comment on stories posted to the site. In the reputation business, that could be *Advertising Age* in the United States or *PR Week* in the UK. Also explore communities such as those on LinkedIn: some are incredibly active. If you post a question about an issue such as which is the best clipping agency or what is the best wire service, you will find that you are inundated with responses in short order. The point is that, if you join in conversations and contribute your own content, you will make new connections and your profile will develop quickly.

Beyond engagement: participation

So content, in many forms and across many media, is the fuel of your reputation. Applying it to best effect is not just about broadcasting it to whoever will listen. Direct engagement with your audience is the first step on the journey to building your reputation through modern, two-way media. It appeals to a fundamental basic human need to be social, and as media continues to evolve in ways that support sustained dialogue, then the one-way street is likely to lose its appeal.

Not just because old media amounted to audiences being told rather than being engaged, but because communication that fosters strong relationships doesn't really work that way. No one enjoys spending time with an individual that only talks about themselves. Think about the times that you have been stuck in the corner of a room at a party with a self-obsessed individual. How long did it take you to make your excuses and head to the bar, or the bathroom? We all want to share our experiences and our needs.

The same premise applies in organisational communication. If a brand broadcasts to its audience with no effort to engage, the audience will have a very limited attention span. But if, instead, the brand makes an effort to understand the concerns of its audience, and not just entertain and inform them but even inspire them, it will be rewarded with attention. Better still, if it strikes the right chord it will be rewarded with influential recommendation through word-of-mouth endorsement, in all its modern forms.

But while engagement gets them looking and listening, you need to go further to build a more successful kind of influence, one that can be the engine room of brand reputation. Once you have engaged your audience you need to build a relationship based on empathy. A brand must truly understand the needs of its audience and respond accordingly. This is participation: a real, sustained and organic conversation between the brand and its audience in which the brand responds directly to the needs of its audience on the audience's terms.

The 'conversation' at the centre of that participation may take place internally within an organisation; it might happen via a social network such as Twitter or Facebook, or via a form of branded media such as a blog, plus in conventional media too. Wherever and however it happens, building a rapport with your audience won't be easy. But then relationships are rarely straightforward. But it is worth the effort. The benefit of truly participating with your audience is incredibly powerful for brand purposes. It is the root of fostering respect and ultimately building the right reputation, insofar as you can command it.

Is it possible to have such an intimate relationship with an audience? We think so. Every bit of evidence points to the fact that consumers are fixated with media in its many forms, and that brands are of persistent interest to them. Social networking is now one of the biggest occupations on the web. We're approaching the position where more people are on social networks than aren't, and still subscriber numbers continue to grow. Consumer backlashes are frequently predicted around privacy issues on social networks such as Twitter but consumers appear to have accepted that handing over personal data is the price that must be paid for access to services online. Your customers are openly volunteering and sharing their personal information in far more detail than you'll find in any customer questionnaire. Corporate computer systems aren't sophisticated enough to harness this information. Very few brands are able to even begin to understand their customers in such a granular level; but that will change in the next decade.

The future of organisational communication, and therefore the future of reputation management, lies in participation of the brand with its audience. That is achieved by understanding the audience and building editorial influence across all forms of applicable media. This should start with a detailed planning exercise to identify and understand your audience, and then build an editorial content plan that forms the basis of engagement, and beyond that, participation.

Then determine the best ways to communicate with your audience. That will almost certainly involve direct engagement with via social forms of media but it will almost certainly include indirect forms of communication via actual discussion, more conventional forms of media, owned or branded media outlets and integration with other forms of marketing.

Again, the simple fact is that you can no longer control your reputation for the simple reason that it isn't yours to control. If you thought you were once in control of it, you're kidding yourself. But you have more chance than ever of being aware of conversations that are taking place about your brand and that provides you with the means to take action to improve or address challenges to your reputation. Your audience wants some type of engagement with you and is almost certainly actively identifying itself on the Internet. For the time being, the measurement of reputation by tangible commercial returns remains a work in progress that is occupying some of the smartest minds in the public relations industry. It is not yet possible to assign a financial value to the impact of a single piece of content about your organisation such as an article online, blog post or a tweet, but the measurement of reputation is becoming more sophisticated and scientific.

Our advice is to stop worrying about whether or not you can control your reputation. You can't. But it needn't be brand anarchy either. Invest your energy in identifying and listening to your audience. Then plan how you will orchestrate the right conversations for your brand in order to engage and participate.

Oh, and get on with it. You haven't much time.

Summary

- Communication practitioners must learn new skills in order to thrive in the new Internet-driven communication environment.
- For now the public relations industry remains wedded to media relations as a means of reaching audiences as a proxy for direct communication with its community.
- The public relations industry is not a profession by the standards of other professions. It lacks the discipline of professional training and enforced continuous professional development.
- The web lowers the cost of access to education and provides the tools for a motivated individual to develop digital skills.
- As our lives and business move online individuals should consider developing and managing their web profile.
- Social networks enables anyone to establish relations and build a personal network online.
- The future of organisational communication lies in participation between an organisation and its markets.

INDEX